AF605038

This boke is one thing
The halter another;
He that stealeth the one
May be sure of the other.

Outré Journal

ISBN 978-0-9751078-6-7 – Soft cover – 1st printing – October, 2012
Editor: Martin McIntosh
Contributors: Brian Chidester, Jean-Emmanuel Deluxe, Martin McIntosh, Boyd Rice, Charles Schneider, Nicholas Syracuse

Typesetting: Trevor Slabak
Layout and design: Trevor Slabak and Martin McIntosh
Cover lettering: Corey Simons – www.thefold.com.au
Cover photograph by Paul Huf - used by kind permission of Maria Austria Instituut
Black House photographs © Nicholas Syracuse
Il Vittoriale and d'Annunzio photos courtesy Il Vittoriale
Select four eyed figures from the collection of and photography: Gregg Gibbs
Grotesque ashtray photography: Alex Aurichio
Other photography: Jeremy Dillon – The Photography Department
Images from the collections of the respective authors' collections unless noted.
Photo 101, 105 (bottom), 110 – courtesy of Jérôme Simon – photobigbang.com
While every effort has been made to trace the original producers of some uncredited art and photos herein, if any have not been credited properly or inadvertently overlooked, the publishers will be pleased to acknowledge them in any future editions of this book.

Thank you: Trevor Slabak for all his hard work on the book, Gemma Jones for her suggestions with text, Corey Simons, Mike and Floor of fotofloor, Glenn Bray, Jérôme Simon, Tony Aguirre, Karin Buchbinder, Grux, Elena Zanini from Il Vittoriale, Patricia Pince van der Aa from Maria Austria Instituut, Kylie McShane, everyone at Outré Gallery, Kristine Anstine, Colin Turner and all at Last Gasp, Claire Thompson, Saraid Banahan.
Special thank you and dedication to April, Edward and Louise McIntosh.

Printed by Prolong Press, China.
Distributed in the US by Last Gasp, 777 Florida St, San Francisco, CA 94110, USA. www.lastgasp.com
Distributed in the UK and Europe by Turnaround Publisher Services, Tel: 020 8829 3002 / email: orders@turnaround-uk.com
Distributed in Australia by Thames & Hudson Australia
Published by Outré Gallery Press, G.P.O. Box 5442, Melbourne, VIC 3001, AUSTRALIA. www.outregallery.com

CONTENTS

Outré

Oratory

outré \oo-TRAY\ , adjective:

Unconventional; eccentric; bizarre.

French, from past participle of outrer to go beyond, carry to excess, from Old French ultrer, utrer, from ultre, outre beyond.

First Known Use: 1722

Synonyms: bizarre, bizarro, cranky, crazy, curious, eccentric, erratic, far-out, funky, funny, kinky, kooky (also kookie), offbeat, off-kilter, outlandish, out-of-the-way, odd, peculiar, quaint, queer, queerish, quirky, remarkable, screwy, spaced-out, strange, wacky (also whacky), way-out, weird, weirdo, wild.

Such a lovely and inspiring word. Following in a worthy tradition, we've taken up the term as our title and catchword. Like those before us we fall under an umbrella of publications that exist outside of the ordinary. The first English publication taking up the title *Outré* which we're aware of was a *Weird Tales* / Lovecraftian fanzine created by Francis Litz who published at least four issues in the late 1930s. Another *Outré*, focusing on all things S&M, was released in the 1940s. And then, in 1963 a different *Outré* fanzine, this one covering the sci-fi and horror genre, was put out by Allen C. Kracalik, and is known to have run for three issues. The most recent, and best known *Outré*, was the professional magazine covering "ultra-media" that was published by the folks who produced *Filmfax* magazine. With a respectful nod to those who came before we carry on the torch with *Outré Journal*.

As with these previous publications, each having their own spin on the name, so too you find with *Outré Journal*. Whilst we do love words, it is pictures that are our forté. The photos, paintings and images within these covers are to be viewed, pondered and appreciated. They might even assist in transporting you to another time, and another place. The outré regions...

True to our name, we are approaching the publication of *Outré Journal*, in our very own way - both in format and contents. Inspired by other publications that came before us such as Charles Addams' *Dear Dead Days*, *The Saturday Book*, and *Pop Void*, we bring you an eclectic mix in a way that uses the loose sense of the term "journal". Due to the sometimes esoteric nature of our contents, one might nowadays expect what you will see here to be on a web log on the internet. We like to emphasize that there are innumerable topics, strangeness and wonder that elude the internet, and can only be found by turning to one's bookshelf. There are outré secrets that reside on the edges of culture, away from the digital pool of accepted knowledge.

Whether it be an old photo or an "out of date" vinyl LP, a good portion of material herein might be looked at as forgotten ephemera, discarded pop culture, or just areas that have never been given the full attention they deserve.

Just as there was talk of the death of vinyl, there is much talk in recent times of the death of print. Our preference is for a physical object, a book in our case. Everything within these pages is best enjoyed in its offset printed form rather than a RGB screen or plastic electronic reading device. The cover is something that needs to be stared at and enjoyed - on a coffee table or proudly displayed on a bookshelf (cover out of course)! It's an object not just to be read, but also admired in person. Take it on a train ride to dazzle and confound those around you with our compelling cover featuring a photo taken in 1956 by Dutch photographer Paul Huf.

Outré Journal is best enjoyed with a drink (and optional pipe) in hand in your favorite lounge chair.

Martin McIntosh
Editor

ɔove and right) Covers of some of our outré pre-
ːcessors. (below) In 1935 *Everyday Science and*
echanics magazine predicted this as the reader of
ᵉ future. We would take this over current electronic
ading devices.

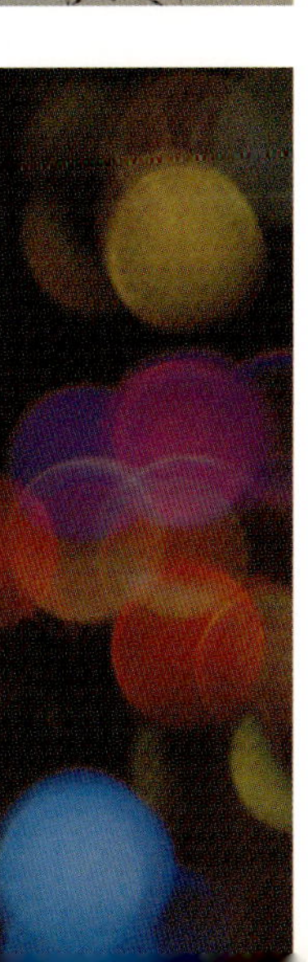

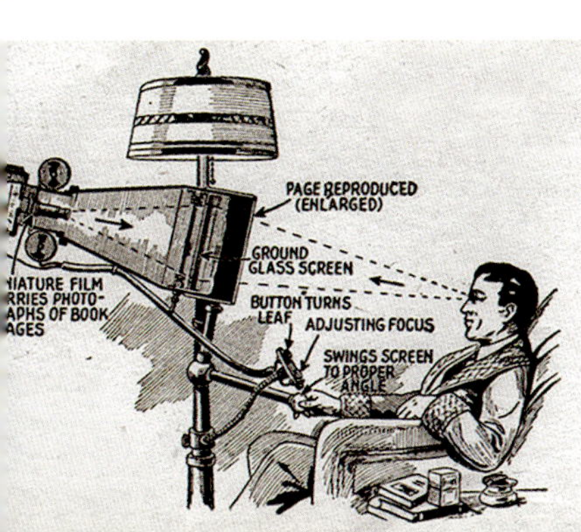

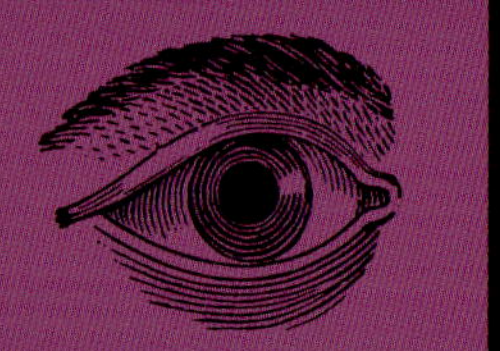

SELECTIONS from the OUTRÉ LIBRARY...

The Dream King
POP VOID #1
Pop Void Publications
DEAR DEAD DAYS
Chas Addams
PUTNAM
BIZARRE
COMPILED BY BARRY HUMPHRIES
ELEK

The Saturday Book

Vincent Price

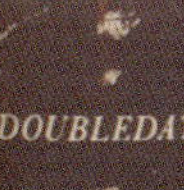

DOUBLEDAY

SECRET
SOCIETIES
EISNER
ARKON DARAUL

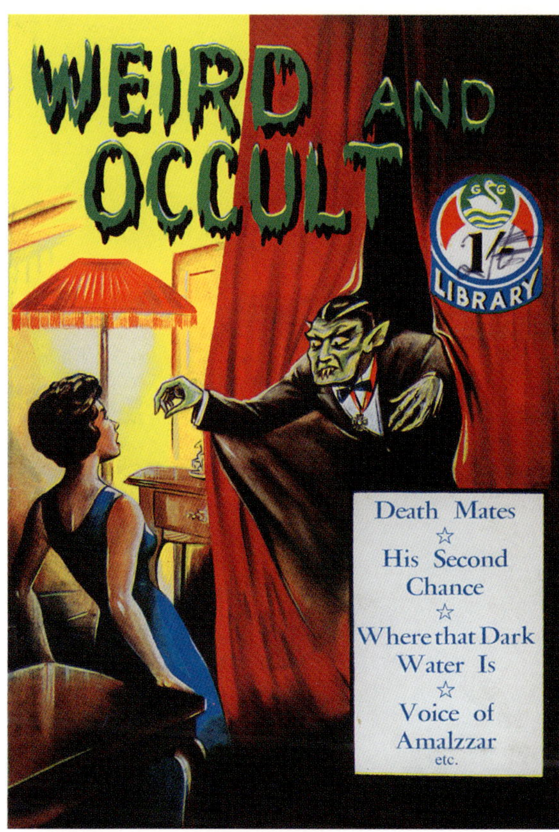
WEIRD AND
OCCULT
1/-
LIBRARY
Death Mates
☆
His Second
Chance
☆
Where that Dark
Water Is
☆
Voice of
Amalzzar
etc.

COOKING
TO KILL!
The Poison Cook-book
SALT
ARSENIC
PEPPER
Concocted by Prof. Ebenezer Murgatroyd
With Comic Drawings by HERB ROTH!

THE
EVIL EYE
Studies in the Folklore of Vision
Edward S. Gifford, Jr., M.D.

JAMES DARK SERIES
Terrifying Tales
HORWITZ
3'9

the zebra-striped hearse
a new, powerful and fast-paced novel by the author of
THE WYCHERLY WOMAN and THE FERGUSON AFFAIR
ROSS MACDONALD

DARKER THAN YOU THINK
Jack Williamson

THE HELLFIRE CLUB
HORWITZ
5'-
The rise and fall of a shocking secret society whose sole interests were perversion and politics

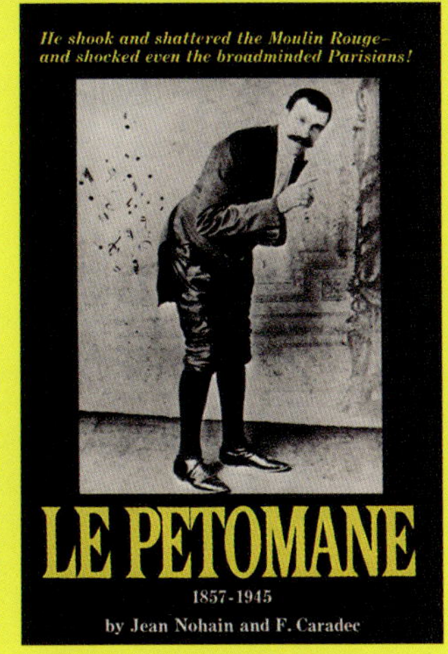

He shook and shattered the Moulin Rouge–
and shocked even the broadminded Parisians!
LE PETOMANE
1857-1945
by Jean Nohain and F. Caradec

by Jackie Kannon
50¢
POEMS
FOR
THE
JOHN

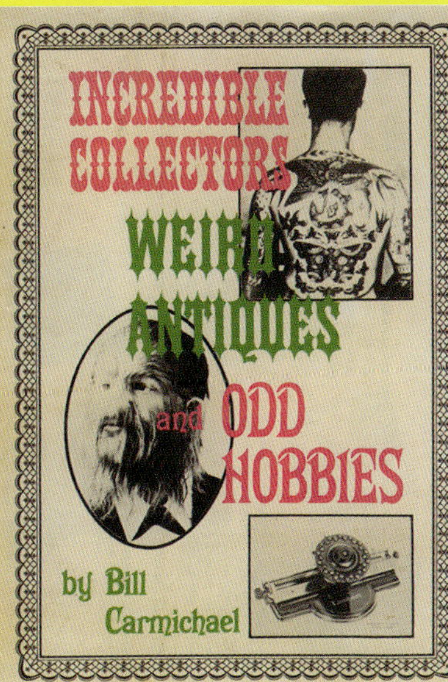

INCREDIBLE COLLECTORS
WEIRD ANTIQUES
and ODD HOBBIES
by Bill Carmichael

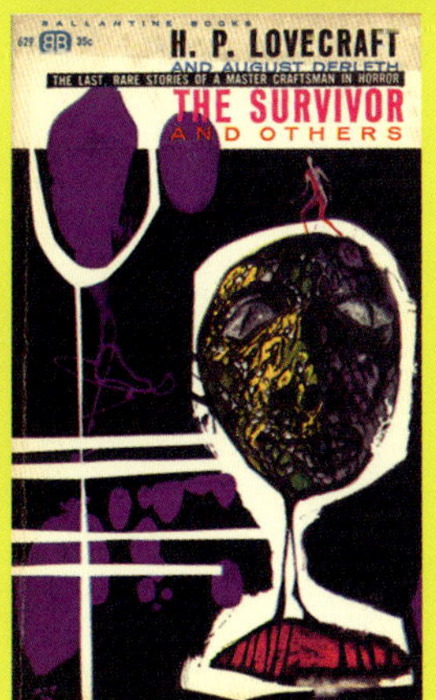

BALLANTINE BOOKS
H. P. LOVECRAFT
AND AUGUST DERLETH
THE LAST RARE STORIES OF A MASTER CRAFTSMAN IN HORROR
THE SURVIVOR
AND OTHERS

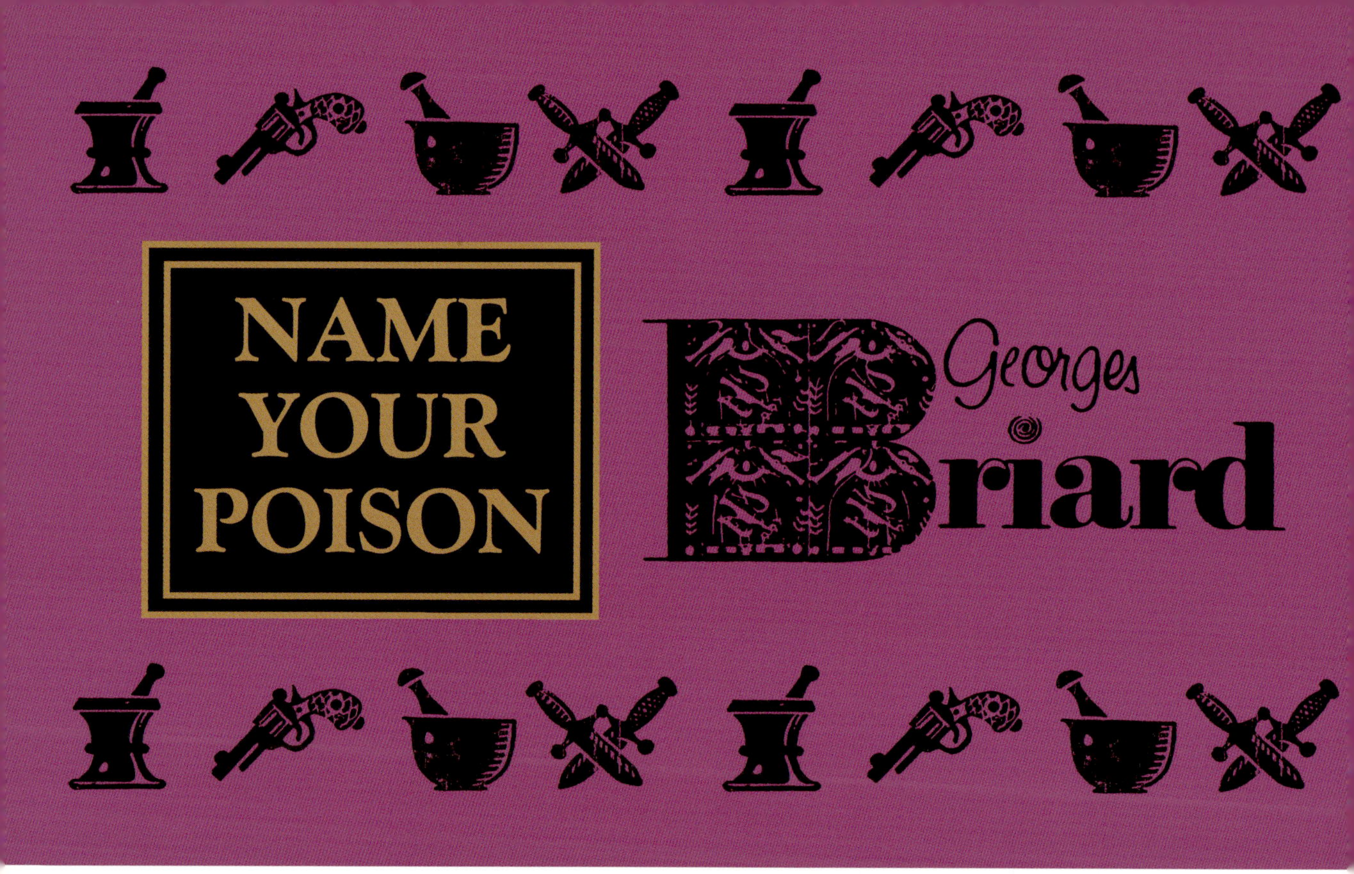

NAME YOUR POISON

Fancy a drink? A little bored with the usual fare? Here's a serving suggestion with a twist... the "Name Your Poison" cocktail set designed by Georges Briard.

Georges Briard (born Jascha Brojdo in the Ukraine in 1917) was a prolific designer working in mid-century America. In 1937 he moved to Chicago where he studied at the Art Institue of Chicago, and then served in the U.S. Army during World War II under General Patton. After the war, he began to paint metal serving trays which is when he started using the name Georges Briard on his commercial work (he was also a painter and signed his fine art Brojdo).

As Georges Briard he designed an impressive range of signature dish ware and glassware which were sold at high profile department stores including Neiman Marcus and Bonwit Teller. The "Name Your Poison" set first released in the 1960s is our favorite Briard design. A glassware collection for those with a dark sense of humor. The whole package for the discerning cocktail set – matching highball tumblers, shots, and mixing pitcher, all served up on "Poison Server" cocktail tray. Each glass is emblazoned with the "Name Your Poison" moniker along the bottom together with pistol, crossed knives, mortar and pestle, and topped off with a delightfully diabolical grinning skull and crossbones.

Briard passed away in 2005 at the age of 88 in New York City. We like to think he might have taken his last drink from one of these.

Bartend, I'll have a double cyanide on the rocks. Now drink up!

Rx Rx
PARIS GREEN
NAME YOUR POISON

Rx Rx
WOOD ALCOHOL
NAME YOUR POISON

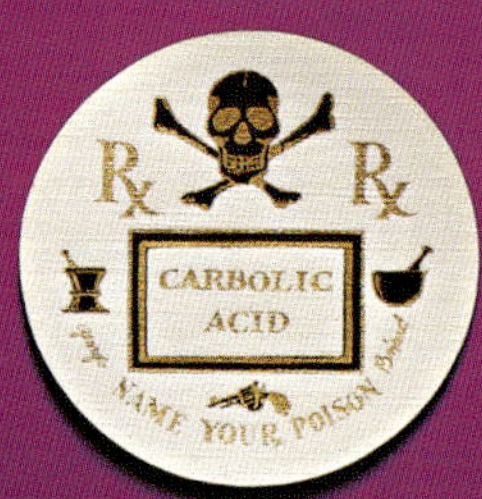
Rx Rx
CARBOLIC ACID
NAME YOUR POISON

Rx Rx
POTASSIUM CYANIDE
NAME YOUR POISON

Rx Rx
POISON SERVERx

Rx Rx
STRYCH-NINE
NAME YOUR POISON

Rx Rx
IODINE
NAME YOUR POISON

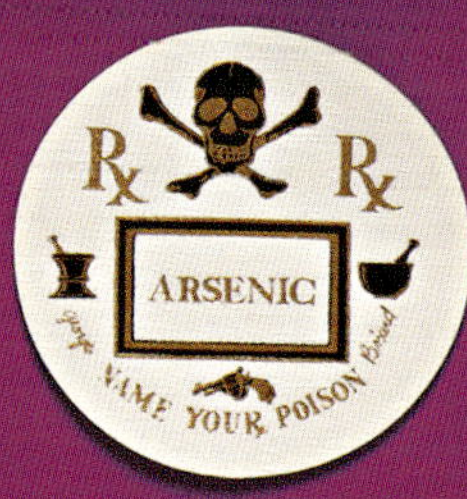
Rx Rx
ARSENIC
NAME YOUR POISON

Rx Rx
NITRO-GLYCERIN
NAME YOUR POISON

POISON
LABORATORY

BLEND YOUR
POISON

BLEND YOUR
POISON

Designer: unknown
Eduard van Beinum conducting the
Concertgebouw Orchestra of Amsterdam
Richmond High Fidelity / London Records

THE ART OF SYMPHONIE FANTASTIQUE

BY MARTIN MCINTOSH

Mostly relegated to under the counter bargain bins and the backs of second hand record stores is the classical music LP. It is perhaps the last bastion in music collecting for great cheap finds and under appreciated album cover artworks.

The album cover, as it is known today, was invented by illustrator Alex Steinweiss. In 1940 he proposed to replace the previously almost universally standard form of packaging a record in a plain sleeve, with an illustrated cover. In no time, recorded music sales jumped by 800 per cent, and a new art form was born. The way records were packaged would never be the same again. Steinweiss lit the creative flame that would be carried on by other artists and designers from then on.

Unlike pop music covers, which generally showed their performers on their fronts, classical music covers took a different approach. There might be depictions (photographic or illustrative) of the composer or conductor. Not necessarily the best way to attract a buyer's attention. Another approach was to reproduce an existing painting from art history that might capture the mood of the music therein. These two options provided adequate housing, and certainly a visual improvement on the plain brown sleeves that had previously been used. However it was a third type of cover that offered a more exciting and fresh approach – that of a contemporary illustration or photograph to convey the theme or mood of the music itself.

Of this last genre, I believe no cover art is richer in aesthetic beauty and wild imagination than *Symphonie Fantastique*, written by French Romantic composer Hector Berlioz in 1830. The subject matter of the symphony lends itself to wondrous and outré interpretations. The story, detailed in Berlioz's program notes, tells of a musician/artist with a lively mind. He poisons himself with opium in despair of a hopeless love. The dose, too small to be fatal, transports him into a deep sleep, broken by strange nightmares including one where he is hanged on a scaffold. The symphony is made up of five movements each with a specific theme, being: "The Passions", "A Ball", "Scene in the Fields", "March to the Scaffold" and "Dreams of a Witches' Sabbath".

Most of the covers to follow were created in the late 1940s through to the late 1960s – a particularly fertile period for illustration and design. And given the florid themes at hand it is not surprising that so many wonderful covers blossomed in the name of this piece of music during this period.

This curated selection features some of the most interesting covers for *Symphonie Fantastique*. Amongst these sparkling gems is one by artist Jane Sinnickson, wife of the late great Jim Flora, on RCA Victor. Research hasn't uncovered any further cover art by Sinnickson, but even if it was the only she ever created it will forever be a masterpiece. The cover's Siamese twin style double-headed, three-eyed woman is a striking and evocative image demanding the viewer's attention. Reputedly it was inspired as her tribute to actress Henrietta Smithson, first wife of Berlioz, and the original inspiration for *Symphonie Fantastique*.

Another fine example, also on RCA Victor, was executed by legendary science fiction artist and illustrator Richard Powers. It features his trademark abstract shapes and evocative swirls of color, perfectly conjuring up an otherworldly mood. Other selections here are photographic offering distorted and surreal settings alluding to the effects of opium and the dream state.

A number of these have been re-issued with lovely reproduction - worth tracking down for the artwork alone. Other covers are rarer due to lesser circulation or having country specific releases such as a Dutch recording on Fontana by The Hague Philharmonic Orchestra. The artwork to this record is a painting depicting a foreboding moonlight landscape populated by spirits in dance and a procession of cloaked figures centered around an enormous guillotine, as detailed in the symphony.

Whether rare or not so, all here are selected for their particular outré quality, and viewed together or individually offer a wonderful visual complement to Berlioz's essential piece of music.

Designer and photographer: unknown
Pierre Monteux conducting the Vienna Philharmonic Orchestra.
RCA Victor

Artwork: Jean Cayré
Pierre Monteux conducting the Orchestre Philharmonique de Vienne
RCA (France)

Artwork and designer: unknown
Pierre-Michel Le Conte conducting the Orchestra of the Paris Opéra
Concert Hall

Photographer: Ingi, montage: Lefor-Openo
Hermann Scherchen conducting the London Symphony Orchestra
Pye

Photographer: David Huorn
Eduard van Beinum conducting the Concertgebouw Orchestra of Amsterdam
Decca Record Company

Artwork and designer: unknown
Sir Eugene Goossens conducting the London Symphony Orchestra
Hallmark Records

Artwork: Ibottiau
Ataulfo Argenta conducting the
Orchestre de la Société des Concerts du Conservatoire de Paris
Decca Disques

Designer and photographer: unknown
Ataulfo Argenta conducting the
Paris Conservatoire Orchestra
London Records

Design: Ronald Clyne
Artur Rodzinski conducting the
Cleveland Orchestra
Columbia Records

Artwork and designer: unknown
Carlo Zecchi conducting the Czech Philharmonic Orchestra
Supraphon

Artwork: Richard Powers
Charles Munch conducting the Boston Symphony Orchestra
RCA Victor

Photographer: Erich Locker
Eugene Ormandy conducting the
Philadelphia Orchestra
Columbia Records

Artwork: Maas
Antal Dorati conducting the
Minneapolis Symphony Orchestra
Mercury Records

Artwork: Joe Weitz
Igor Markevitch conducting the
Berlin Philharmonic Orchestra
Decca Records

Photographer: Alfred Wertheimer
Pierre-Michel Le Conte conducting the
Orchestre du Théâtre de l'Opera, Paris
Columbia Records

Artwork: unknown
Willem van Otterloo conducting the Hague Philharmonic Orchestra
Fontana

Artwork: Stanley / Monogram
Eugene Ormandy conducting the Philadelphia Orchestra
Columbia Records

Designer and photographer: unknown
Antal Dorati conducting the Minneapolis Symphony Orchestra
Pickwick International

Artwork: Bruno
Igor Markevitch conducting the Orchestre Philharmonique de Berlin
Deutsche Grammophon

Artwork: Jane Sinnickson
Charles Munch conducting the Boston Symphony Orchestra
RCA Victor

Artwork: Goaman
Eduard van Beinum conducting the
Concertgebouw Orchestra of Amsterdam
Decca Record Company

Designer: Fritz Huber
Wladimir Golschmann conducting the
Orchester der Wiener Staatsoper in der Volksoper
Amadeo

Artwork and designer: unknown
André Cluytens conducting the
Orchestre National de la Radiodiffusion Française
Columbia Records

Artwork and designer: unknown.
Igor Markewitch conducting
Orchester Lamoureux Paris
Eterna

Who is Knud Albert?

by Martin McIntosh

Very little is known about the Danish artist and designer who stamped his peculiar wooden creations Knud Albert.

Presented here is a selection of his work dating from the 1950s and 1960s.

Albert sits within the world of other Danish mid-century designers such as Kristian Vedel and Kay Bojesen, who crafted stylized animals out of wood. Whereas specific characters are easily identified in Vedel and Bojesen's output, Albert's work departs from these designers by way of their peculiarly outré nature. His creations are without doubt out of the ordinary and often defy categorization.

His known works are predominantly executed in teak and rosewood, the two woods most common to Danish Modern furniture. Legend has it that Albert would obtain the wood for his sculptures from the discarded off-cuts of various Danish furniture makers prolific from the post World War II era through the early 1970s. Recycling random off-cuts might explain the uniquely distorted and odd formations of most of Albert's creations.

Known examples of his work indicate that he had a range of recurring characters including elongated dog-like creatures, beaked and long legged martian-esque teak and fur beings, and tall eared cartoonish rabbits. Even within these repeated characters there is a beautiful degree of individuality and variation.

And then there are Albert's other creations that defy categorization - biomorphic warped, deformed and delightful. All characteristically Knud Albert - these unique creatures of wood sit somewhere between toys and fine art; cartoons and craft; surrealism and folk-art.

Albert's anthropomorphized wooden creatures have a particularly Scandinavian resonance. His creatures' personality and likeness have something of a kinship with the characters dreamt by Tove Jansson. Odd blobs with minimal facial features. Beaky beings with a tinge of folklore.

It is not surprising that these figures sit perfectly within a mid-century styled setting. One might view them as the negative spaces left from some

of the nicest Danish furniture of the time. They are crafted with the same materials and with a similar attention to detail and finish. They are like the impish flipside, hiding in the shadows, of some of the most sought after home furnishings.

To hold them is to appreciate their light, fragile beauty, and to confirm their firm status as objects other than toys.

Albert flies under the historic radar, and little is spoken of this ingenious craftsman. It is only in the past few years that rare snippets have appeared online. The most detailed account referencing the man himself comes from a contributor to a weblog (http://findingthegrail.wordpress.com) who writes:

I lived in Denmark during 1964/5 and met Knud Albert while visiting H.C. Anderson's home in Odense on the island of Fyn. I can't remember how it came about ... I think he may have had the wooden animals in a shop there but somehow my friend and I ended up meeting him. We both loved his work but were poor students and couldn't afford most of the prices so he took us back into his storage area and let us buy some of his "seconds"... which were really in great shape. He was a lovely warm man, as you might expect from his wonderful creatures, and we had a great visit with him. My guess is that he was in his 40's at that time. We were traveling on our bikes and so we didn't have room to buy much, but I still have a couple of his creatures and am happy other people are also enjoying them.

Let's hope more information comes to hand on this hereto forgotten craftsman, and the mystery of Knud Albert the designer and artist untwists.

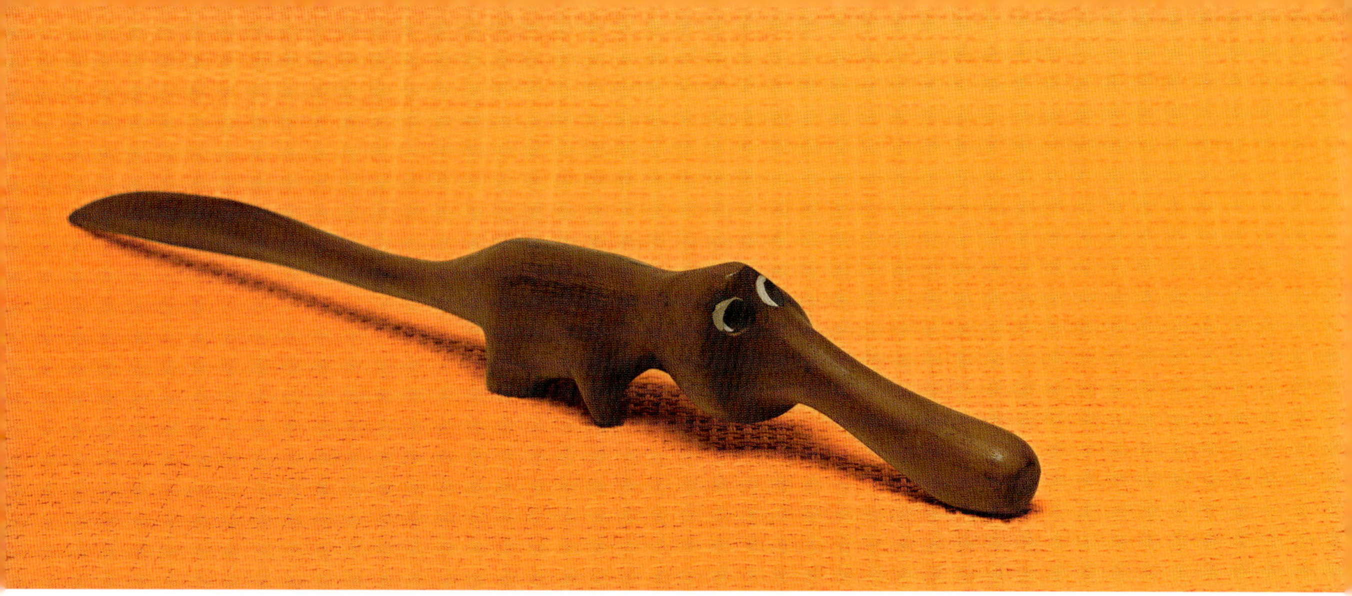

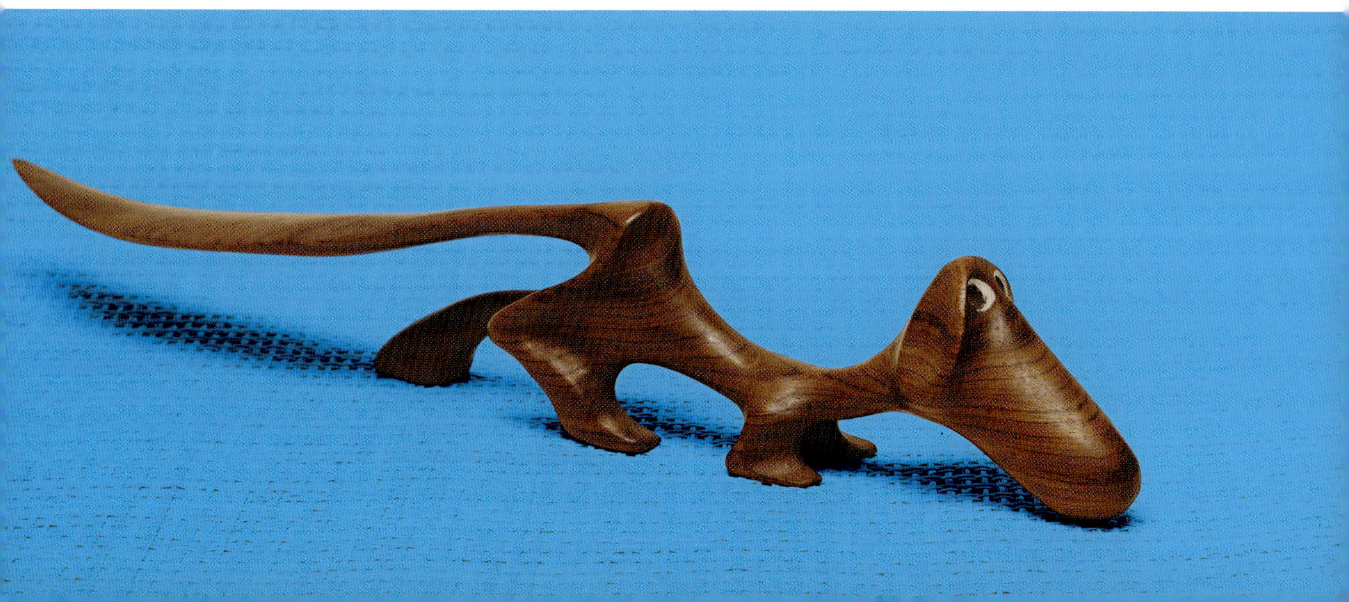

ALP 1013
PANAMA
PANAMA ARTISTS INC. TRADE MARK REG.
SATAN TAKES A HOLIDAY
$ 3.98
FEATURING THE PIANO STYLING OF
BUDDI SATAN
HI FIDELITY RECORDING
TURNIP GREEN • DRUMS
JIMMY WOODE • BASS
WALFREDO REYES JR. • TIMBALES
BILL ALVEREZ • BONGOS

when sin was FUN

by boyd rice

decades before the artist Coop, the seductive devil girl was a potent symbol of lust and temptation. Part of her allure was undoubtedly that because she was an embodiment of sin and carnality, she also symbolized the imagined fulfillment of the same lust and temptation. Sure, you'd catch a glimpse of her in the day's men's magazines, but she was just as likely to be seen in the mainstream media; on billboards or in supermarkets. She had horns, a skin-tight red cat-suit and a come hither look. In one hand was a pitchfork, in the other a product. For mainstream America, the Devil Girl was both a symbol of longing and a symbol of fun. And in an uptight era, fun was a powerful inducement!

She was used to sell everything from Gin to heat lamps. In a Smirnoff ad that appeared in the sixties, one such vixen holds aloft a cocktail in one hand and in the other a pitchfork upon which two large ice cubes are impaled. The copy reads:

"The Smirnoff Martini. A devilishly dry proposition. Compared to Smirnoff, any other kind of "dry" is all wet. Make a pact to have one tonight."

Whoa! Can you imagine any mainstream magazine running such an ad today? Hardly, but in the sixties Satan was sexy. A great many people undoubtedly knew that there was forbidden fruit out there to be had, but the lion's share had yet to taste it.

Enter: Satanica, a marketing device whose appeal was directed toward the pleasures of the flesh. Desire, excess, gratification... all yours – for a price. You want it, don't you?

In retrospect, it seems ironic that in an age so defined and dominated by Judeo-Christian values, that Madison Avenue's satanic seduction was not only tolerated, but found amusing by mainstream America. Most people (Christians and Atheists) seemed far less uptight then.

The devil was used to hawk everything from adult paperbacks to albums of easy listening music; and for several decades even a delightfully frothy drink called Orange Julius. Orange Julius stores were a staple in virtually every suburban mall in the United States, and emblazoned on the store's façade was the figure of a red devil and the slogan "A Devilish Good Drink". Such satanic imagery was phased out in the '80s but remained on most stores for many years thereafter. A similar devil still adorns cans of Underwood Deviled Ham, just as it has for decades.

For a brief time there was even a men's magazine called *Satan*, catering to the discriminating bachelor. The editorial page bore the slogan "abandon hope, all ye who enter here", and usually consisted of a few paragraphs extolling the virtues of the rogue male superimposed over a woodcut of orgiastic "witches sabbats", or Gustave Dore depictions of souls writhing in Hell.

The magazine's mascot was no fuzzy bunny, but rather a sophisticated Mephistopheles; decked out in a tux, with the legs of a goat and cloven hooves.

Another similar magazine published just a few years later was called *Satana*. While less thorough going in its satanic theme, the content was bawdier, the models more lustful seeming. What it lacked in terms of high concept, it more than made up for in carnal content. And that, after all, is the raison d'être of Satanica.

Around the same time there appeared on the market "The Devils Potion", a set of fragrances for men. Its slogan was "Scent from the Devil to You". The gift box looked like some infernal necronomicon, the cover emblazoned with flames and sulphurous red billowing clouds of smoke. Inside was an "After Shave Potion" and "Cologne for Devilish Men". All in all, a great idea for a father's day gift. The text on the inside cover says it all:

"There's a little of the devil in every man. But most men could use a lot more. Because if you're too good, life can be dull. But if you're devilish, life can be interesting..."

The text went on to say that the Devil's Potion could bring out the devil in any man, and – oh yeah – it's for external use only; keep out of the reach of children and "avoid use near an open flame".

For a time there were Satan themed cocktail lounges, such as the Devil's Den at the Devil's Head ski resort in Devils Head, Wisconsin. It was a vision in red, what with red leather booths, red walls and ceilings – all illuminated by the eerie glow of red recessed lighting. The men's room was labeled "Devils", the ladies room "Witches". The place, I'm told, was still in existence as late as the mid – '90s; but sadly, a quick glance at the internet announces the "newly remodeled" Devil's Den, which looks like a brew pub at the airport. At one time, there were a few devil themed nightspots in the Big Apple. One, in Harlem, had guests descend

via slide into a red hued basement replicating the underworld – complete with live jazz and dancing. But the roots of satanic nightlife go much further back than '50s cocktail lounges or the jazz age.

In the Fin de siècle Paris of the 1800s, there was a bar called Le Enfer (The inferno, or Hell). Its façade was a massive sculpture of the face of the Devil, shrieking; and one entered through his mouth. At this entrance was a doorman attired as Satan, complete with a pitchfork in one hand. Once inside, the devilish theme continued. A good many of the drinks contained brimstone (i.e. sulphur) as a main ingredient. Others simply had chunks of dry ice tossed in to make them bubble and boil. In the entrance hall was a vast

cauldron in which a near naked woman appeared to be being cooked alive as part of the ambience.

In a small room off to one side, a display took place every hour on the hour. Behind a wall of glass, a man opened a coffin to reveal what appeared to be the pale cadaver of a beautiful young woman. As the light began to shift and change, the woman's flesh appeared to shrivel and crack. Soon it faded altogether and only a skeleton remained – to both the horror and delight of onlookers. It was a simple but effective illusion, achieved through the use of colored lights and mirrors. What boggles the mind is that such fare was mainstream entertainment in the 1890s, and I seriously doubt that there's a watering hole existent today that could hold a candle to it.

Satanica, as such, no longer exists. As a genre, it is as dead as the dodo. More's the pity.

At the height of the Haight Ashbury period in the '60s a badge was produced, boldly announcing (in psychedelicized typeface) that "SIN IS IN". Paradoxically, it was probably the widespread acceptance of such an attitude that spelled the beginning of the end of Satanica. With large segments of the culture growing ever increasingly tolerant and accepting of lust, carnality, free love, et al; the notion of sin was vanishing. In point of fact, sin was out.

Without the concept of sin, the notion of forbidden fruit withered on the vine and died a death. And gone with it was the very idea of temptation, along with all of the voluptuous devil girls coyly tempting us to yield to it – and them. Frankly, I miss them.

THE MAGAZINE FOR THE MAN ABOUT TOWN
Debonair
Articles • Fiction
Cartoons • Photography

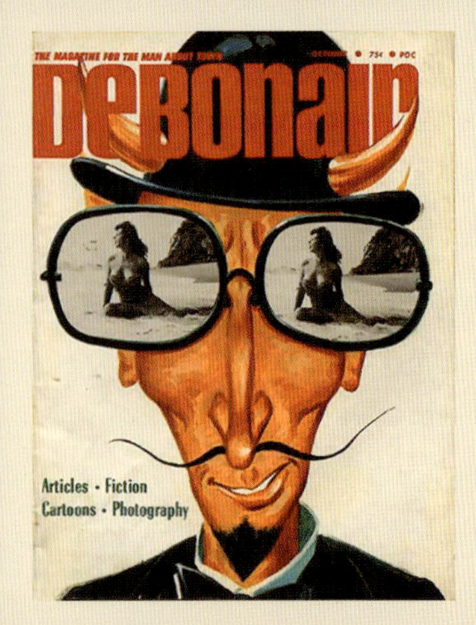

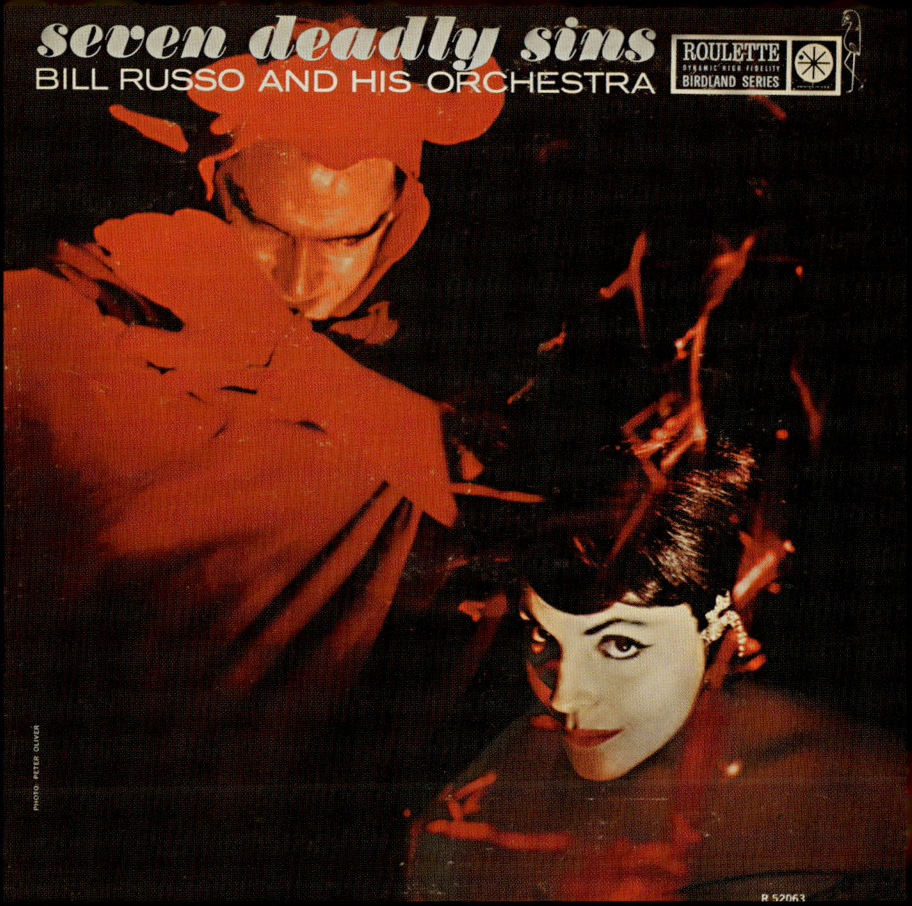

seven deadly sins
BILL RUSSO AND HIS ORCHESTRA
ROULETTE
DYNAMIC HIGH FIDELITY
BIRDLAND SERIES
PHOTO: PETER OLIVER
R 52063

Diabolical

A DELL BOOK
DELL
415
Eve, Salome, Helen of Troy, Delilah, and other gay lovelies confess all...
LADIES IN HADES
Frederic Arnold Kummer

SYLVANIA
heat lamp
thaws • soothes • dries

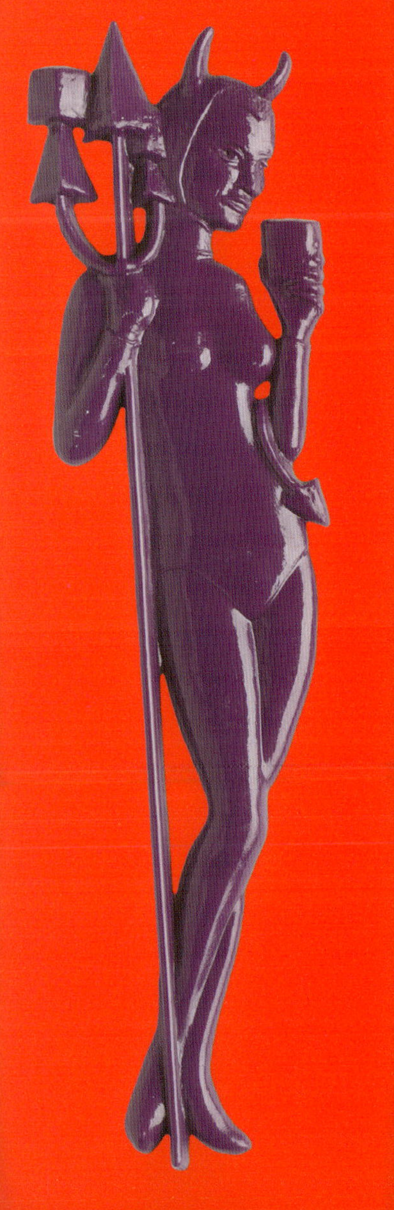

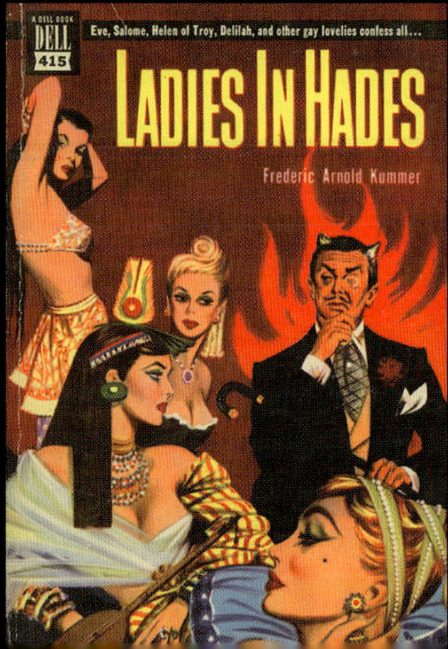

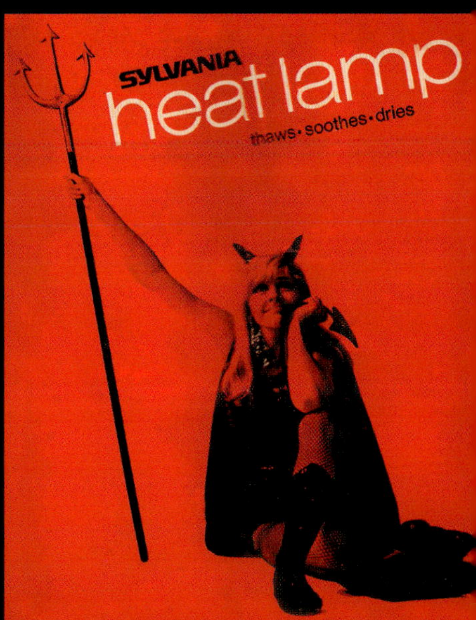

Man about Town
fiction, photography, articles, ribaldry

original soundtrack
satan in HIGH HEELS
starring MEG MYLES – SABRINA
conducted and composed by
MUNDELL LOWE
PARKER

Satanica!

satan

the Hollywood Playboys Orchestra
directed by Mahlon Merrick
RUSS TAYLOR
The "Sportsmen" Quartette
URANIA
UR 9012
SYMBOL OF HIGH FIDELITY
Music for Playboys to Play By

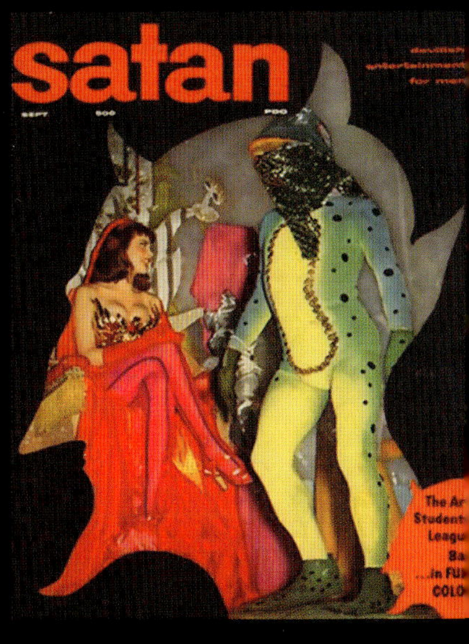

WeiRDSViLLe...

THE WORLD OF THE BEATNIK

Raymond Bowley Sing, Sausalito Girls, 1965, oil on panel in custom made frame (wood and velvet), 6 x 6 1/4" /15cm x 16cm
opposite – clockwise from top left) Like Man – Me Worry? postcard / found photo / found photo / Écoute Ce Disque EP cover

GreenWich ViLLage's

Café BIZARRE

PRESENTS

AssorteD MadNess

BEAT GENERATION POETRY

BEAT EROTICA by the

BEAT & THE UNBEAT

reenwich Village's Café Bizarre - LP cover

pposite – clockwise from top left) *Sick Along With Us* - LP cover / photographic still / *A Real Gone Goose* by George Bagby / beachnik towel

STRAND
SLP 1009
SICK ALONG WITH US
the GROUP THERAPISTS
TGT
TGT
PSYCHIATRIC comedy for Cracked POTS
Stall Jacob production

"THROUGH THESE PORTALS PASS THE MOST"

LIKE KEEP COOL MAN!
OFF BEAT POEMS

A REAL GONE GOOSE
George Bagby

(this page) U.S. Air Force Academy Chapel – Colorado Springs.

(opposite) Even Frank Lloyd Wright can go wrong. Wright created many timeless modernist churches during the course of his career. Though this may not be one of them, it is nonetheless a shining example of space age church design. Annunciation Greek Orthodox Church, 1961.

Blast Off!

Religious Architecture in the Space Age

by Boyd Rice

We've all seen them. Strange modernist churches... bygone edifices that even now bear testament to an era in which man seemingly stood on the threshold of conquering outer space. Some such sanctuaries look like flying saucers or dwellings on another planet. Others had roofs so intensely aerodynamic that they looked for all the world as though they could take off and fly. It's probably safe to say that more modernist architecture was commissioned via the auspices of the church than any other single source. It's also a safe bet to assume that these churches and temples probably represented opportunities for a lot of lesser-known architects to flex their creative muscles. The marketplace was very conservative then, and for every superstar architect such as Frank Lloyd Wright there were thousands of others who had to kowtow to their client's pedestrian tastes. It's no wonder then that so many of these architects seem to have put everything they had into a single structure. It may well have been their only shot at such a project.

The inescapable paradox that governs space age church architecture is that the religious orthodoxy of the time undoubtedly adhered to values that were much more conservative in nature than those represented in the architectural marketplace. Why then, the emphasis on radical design, coming from heretofore hardcore traditionalists? What made Catholics, Protestants, Lutherans, Baptists and Jews all want to take a giant leap into the space age (and all at roughly the same time)?

In mid-century America (and indeed across the globe) the notion of the space age was quickly becoming a defining ethic. The future, it seemed, loomed just around the bend. And the road to the future was paved with progress, which was everywhere evident at the time. Man had mastered the atom, was circling the earth in space capsules, and appeared to be reconstructing reality in his own image. He was well on his way to becoming Master of the Universe. Man had gone from the horse and buggy to rocket science in a relatively brief span of time. And by mid-century his technology continued to evolve exponentially. The future was everywhere – all around us.

In Disneyland you could ride a monorail, stroll through the House of the Future, talk on a videophone, or go on a faux "trip to the moon". In your local record shop you could purchase long-playing records of E-Z listening "music from outer space". Each year the new car models looked more and more like they'd been designed by NASA; and even hot rodders like "Big Daddy" Roth jumped on the bandwagon with cars like The Orbitron. In other words, the future was endemic. Inescapable.

The church's adoption of a modernist aesthetic happened on quite a large scale. Most towns have a few examples of space age churches, and most cities probably have numerous examples. In the fifties and sixties there were even ecclesiastic supply houses that put out whole catalogs of modern art vestments in an attempt to keep abreast of the ever burgeoning craze; just as Judaica suppliers mass produced cubist effigies of old testament images such as the burning bush, cast in bronze for display on the front of mod synagogues.

Happily, a great many examples of space age places of worship have withstood the test of time. Some seem as compelling and contemporary today as they must have fifty or sixty years ago. Not surprisingly, there are a good many that seem dated and cheesy. Truth be told, some of these places must have seemed hokey by the standards of the era. More than a few seem influenced by the "Googie" coffee shop design of influential firms like Armet & Davis. Others are little more than rip-offs of the sort of ersatz Polynesian design elements found in tiki hotels and motels at the time. What the latter has to do with the space age is anybody's guess.

Still, these structures polka dot the landscape like the gigantic stone heads of Easter Island. And like those huge heads, they remain an enigma.

(top) Why isn't all modern art this good? The interior of Westminster Presbyterian Church in Youngstown, Ohio.

(above) St Louis Priory Church. Designed by architects Hellmuth, Obata & Kassabaum.

(left) The Jetson's house? Nope. It's "The Prayer Tower" at Oral Roberts University.

(opposite top) Vestments: What the space age clergyman was sporting in 1963.

(opposite below) St George Greek Orthodox Church - Manchester, New Hampshire.

(opposite) Oral Roberts University Prayer Tower during the day. "The 200-foot prayer tower represents a modern-day cross and is crowned by a flame symbolic of the Holy Spirit. Observation level houses the Abundant Life Prayer Group, on duty 24 hours a day".

(above) If there were a chapel at Disneyland, it might look like this. St Januarius Church - The Grape Grotto - Naples, New York.

(left and below) Interior and exterior views of the Grace Lutheran Church – St Petersburg, Florida.

(opposite top left) North Christian Church – Columbus, Indiana. Designed in 1964 by famed Finnish American architect and designer Eero Saarinen, whose other well known designs included the TWA Air Terminal at JFK International, and numerous mid century modern furniture pieces including the Grasshopper chair, the Womb chair, and Tulip chair.

(opposite bottom) The interior of the North Christian Church.

(opposite top right) Ready to launch into orbit? St Charles Parish Church in Spokane, Washington.

(this page) Exterior and interior shots of the New Testament First Christian Church in Brazil, Indiana. Ten years in the planning and it was dedicated in 1966.

(opposite page) For some this exterior image may evoke architecture from *Planet of the Apes*, and the altar might bring to mind the *Star Trek* transporter room. These are in fact exterior and interior shots of St Mary's Church in Red Deer, Alberta.

(above) First Presbyterian Church - Stamford, Connecticut. Architect Wallace Harrison included 20,000 chunks of inch thick glass and 152 pre-cast panels of concrete covered with slate.

(below) Yesterday's vision of Tomorrow. The First Christian Church in Oklahoma City, Oklahoma.

Church of tomorrow

(left) Chapel of the Holy Cross – Sedona, Arizona.

(below) Immanuel Lutheran Church – Broken Arrow, Oklahoma.

(bottom) Dig that crazy stained-glass! St John Ev. Lutheran Church – Brackenridge, Pennsylvania.

(left) Ecclesiastic Mondrian style colored glass from 1962 in the Trinity Lutheran Church – Valley View, Pennsylvania.

(below) Three hyperbolic paraboloid roofs form a canopy over the main alter at the Mary, Queen of Peace Catholic Church in Ulysses, Kansas.

(bottom) St John's Abbey – University Church - Collegeville, Minnesota designed by architect Marcel Breuer.

above) Grace Lutheran Church – University Lutheran Center – State College, Pennsylvania.

below) Mondrian inspired colored glass strikes again! Interior of the First Methodist Church in Mt Pleasant, Michigan.

(opposite top) Grace Lutheran Church – Columbus, Indiana. Designed in 1966 by architectural firm James Associates, two years after Saarinen had designed his space age church in that city.

(opposite bottom) A colored skylight and way out custom light fitting offset the warm wooden tones of this organic modernist space age church. Kalikonani Catholic Church – Puako, Hawaii.

(right) Interior of the Sunny Isles Lutheran Church – Miami Beach, Florida.

(below) Saint-Denys-du-Plateau designed in 1964 by architect Jean-Marie Roy.

GROTESQUE FACIAL ASHTRAYS

by charles schneider

I first learned of these incredible ashtrays while thumbing through an old book, which I'd had since a child. Spinning Wheel's *Antiques For Men* was a book published in 1974. It anthologized a number of articles; all sharing the editor's picks of unique items he felt were particularly masculine collectible objects. These included beer steins, knives, guns, "railroadiana", lead soldiers, snuff boxes, smoking memorabilia, sporting goods, toys, political ephemera, bronze objects and other things that might look good in an oak lined den or smoky hunting lodge. "If he hasn't already started to collect, let him choose one or several of the many interesting collectibles suggested in this book," we are encouraged, both for fun and as an investment.

Only now, forty years later, did a specific article capture my fancy and fill me with that delicious madness which only the incurable curio collector may know.

"Ashtrays with Faces" by Marcia Ray focused on the collection of Robert Jones, a banker and lifelong collector in New York City. As a child Jones collected Cap pistols. In mid-life he moved onto toy banks. Upon retiring, the venerable fellow fixed his sights upon cigars and tobacco memorabilia dating from the 1880s through the early 1900s. When the article was written, Jones was still collecting turn-of-the-century ashtrays, which were cast in "bronze, brass or tin."

"Humor of a rather macabre sort was not neglected; among Mr. Jones rarities are a skeleton, a coffin plate, and a Turkish toilet!"

Although these ashtrays almost never contain the signature of the artist or sculptor, nor the foundry, I have observed that, clearly, one great artist/sculptor was responsible for several of the creations. The more one studies the cute, curl of the crusty fisherman's ear; one may match the style exactly with other ears on other faces. In one instance I found a faint fingerprint on a piece, deep within the brass for over a century.

As Ms. Ray noted, only the ashtrays which carry the name of an advertising company, or product, allow us o date these weird items. She also pointed out that these ashtrays do not seem derived from any pre-existing art. In fact, they seem to have been sculpted with the odd predilections of these unknown artist's whims and fancies, aimed at delighting the smoker in his home. In fact, the ornate details, the grooves and bizarre ornamentations would make them more difficult to clean. An example of form overpowering function in a beautiful and twisted way.

I have noticed one intriguing hint. Several of the ashtrays, which seem to be sculpted by a singular and mercurial artist, bearing a similar style and sculpting technique, share oval shaped tags, or stamps, on their bottoms. The writing is frustratingly indecipherable, but perhaps one day an ashtray may turn up in better condition. This may allow a future Sherlock Holmes of the bizarre to take up the mystery, which I have only just breeched.

Mr. Jones favored specific ashtrays that focused on weird faces. I had to get these things!

I became obsessed with getting as many of the items featured in the article as possible. I was quite successful. One may often find the ashtrays from anywhere between $20 and $200. eBay makes collecting easier, which is both great and sad. The hunt becomes easier. Yet one day the wild and rare weird objects and books of the world may become extinct, even in the electronic realm. Whereas they may have been able to hide out in lonely antique and bookstores for centuries, waiting for the right kind of person to take them home and love them forever. Now – those curio collectors armed with a keen eye and overflowing drool bucket, may ferret out the grotesque gold amongs the dross.

Sometimes one may find the exact same ashtray cas in different materials, say pewter and cheaper aluminum. It seems that there were knock-offs of popular shapes by other firms, which makes collectible myriad variables a fun wrinkle in the mania!

As the world about us becomes colder and uglier, le us rejoice in the creation of our own inner worlds! Le us surround ourselves with precious treasures we have singled out or created ourselves, and shun the plastic hordes of ugliness which the tasteless and the corporate worlds strive to shove down our throats joining the puppet ranks, filling the puppet shelves reading the same puppet books!

I, for one, have found grotesque facial ashtrays as good a place to start as any. Cheers!

(opposite) A superb, bacchanalian devil sculpted by the unknown "master," responsible, I am sure, for several of the very best, most passionately warped ashtrays. He is a cross between a devil, Bacchus and the "green man." He has leafy ears, two cleverly conceived fangs, one on the top and one on the mouth's bottom, and curling eyebrows

(top right) Close up of mystery tag, hinting at the ashtray's origins.
(above left) A ferocious lion, fit for a hunter's trophy room.
(above right) A probable nautical fellow, most likely a jolly fisherman. The handling of the ear suggests it was sculpted by the same artist as some of the other finer ashtrays thus far uncovered.

This leering, curly-haired devil is full of charm and Mephistophelian whimsy. In fact, it has been recast and is available in a rather nice new version with blue glass marble eyes. The maker suggests that it may be used as "an ashtray, a tray for sugar cubes for absinthe, or as a cool addition to your home decor."

Amazing spook face, probably meant to represent a ghost or demonically playful spirit. This was cast in bronze.

(above left) A smaller ashtray featuring a skipper or ship's captain

(above right) A wizened, owl-like gentleman. A delightful and eccentric example of the facial ashtray!

(right) Similar to the "Bacchus-Devil", this grinning and bizarre sun-deity of sorts was surely also sculpted by the unknown "master."

A deep set ashtray sports a particularly grim and vampiric looking bat face. Spooky and truly macabre.

Way out at the Café Frankenstein

By Brian Chidester

No building stands today where once stood the Café Frankenstein in Laguna Beach, California.

A flattened parking lot currently rests over the spot where the coffeehouse formerly nestled up to a hillside overlooking the Pacific Ocean. In an arts community that prides itself on cultural offerings such as the annual Pageant of Masters, the Laguna Art Museum and an artisans boardwalk that features a bazaar of crafts and paintings, this sleepy Southern California hamlet would rather forget the nightmare that was the Café Frankenstein.

(opposite) Anonymous woman dressed in white outside of Café Frankenstein. (Collection of Martin McIntosh).

(left) Doug Myres strums his guitar while Burt Shonberg looks on. (Courtesy of George Clayton Johnson).

(below) Café Frankenstein patrons beat out a bongo beat. Mural by Shonberg in the background. From *Escapade* magazine, December 1959.

The monster was first unleashed in March of 1958. Café Frankenstein was the brainchild of three creative entities: writer George Clayton Johnson, folk singer Doug Myres and painter Burt Shonberg.

"Our goal was perhaps ill-conceived," admits Johnson from his home in the San Fernando Valley. "We created the place in hopes of gathering other outcasts such as ourselves into a creative and open environment."

The tiny wooden structure sat at 860 S. Coast Boulevard, designed (rather basic) by the Bill Bluerock architectural firm, painted black and emblazoned with Burt Shonberg's mural art and stained glass depictions of the Frankenstein monster in a number of empathetic settings.

"Burt wasn't afraid of the monster," recalls Ledru Baker Shoopman III, who was Shonberg's roommate in Seal Beach, California from 1968-77. "I speak of the monster inside us all."

Every square inch of the Café Frankenstein, including a telephone phone pole out front, featured Shonberg artwork. Many of these inscriptions looked like cryptic symbols, Kabalistic letters and amorphic shapes inspired by Seattle artist Mark Tobey, who during the 1940s bridged the gap between abstract expressionism and the simplicity of Far Eastern calligraphy. Covering most of one side of the coffeehouse was Shonberg's massive painting of the Frankenstein monster wearing a spaceman outfit engaged in a serious game of chess. The piece was done on masonite board and mounted to the exterior wall.

No one is sure how Burt came to identify with the monster in so deep a way. But one thing is certain: "Burt saw himself *as* Frankenstein," related Michael Schley, one of the coffeehouse's early baristas. "Café Frankenstein was Burt Shonberg's masterpiece. It was more than just a clever name for a beatnik hotspot."

Indeed, a letter sent by Shonberg to Forrest J. Ackerman, the man who coined the term "Sci-Fi," confirms his kinship to the monster. Addressed 7/15/57 (a full nine months prior to the café's opening), the letter is largely taken up with Shonberg's watercolor painting of the Frankenstein monster, who from the chest up sprouts from a field of flowers. Shonberg painted the monster as Boris Karloff's famous Frankenstein from the Universal Studios film of 1931, offering the same mystic symbols utilized on the exterior of the Café Frankenstein building, here are printed all over the monster's body. There is no separation between the monster and the floral cornucopia around him, every square inch of the painting appearing connected and alive.

A byline across the top of the painting/letter reads:

"Mr. Shonberg and large friend (below) are both available thru the Ackerman Agency.

"Backgrounds: The monster is from the Actors' Studio in New York and also trained occasionally at Stillman's Gym. Burt Shonberg is highly influenced by the Martian School and first began painting while living amongst the Abominable Snowmen of Tibet."

In truth, Shonberg was born on March 30, 1933 in Revere, Massachusetts. He entered the school at the Boston Museum of Fine Arts from 1953-55, then joined the Army in 1956, where he served two years. While painting a mural for his military unit's mess hall, Shonberg claimed he was discovered as an artist. moving to Los Angeles a year later. It was in L.A. that Shonberg met Forrest J. Ackerman and his co-conspirator in the Café Frankenstein, George Clayton Johnson.

A little background on both Ackerman and Johnson seems in order.

"Forry" Ackerman, as his friends liked to call him, was a pioneer in the world of science fiction. Besides being a lifelong nudist and self-ascribed atheist, Ackerman is perhaps best remembered as the founder, publisher and editor of *Famous Monsters of Filmland*, a magazine that celebrated all manner of ghouls, robots

(top) Café Frankenstein ad drawn by Shonberg from *Le Petit Sphinx - The Coffee House Review* (Collection of Martin McIntosh)

(middle) 1930s photo of Shonberg's agent and sci-fi pioneer Forrest J. Ackerman. (Collection of Brian Chidester)

(below) Exterior of Café Frankenstein. (Courtesy of George Clayton Johnson)

(opposite) Letter from Shonberg to Ackerman, circa 1957. (Courtesy of Forrest J. Ackerman)

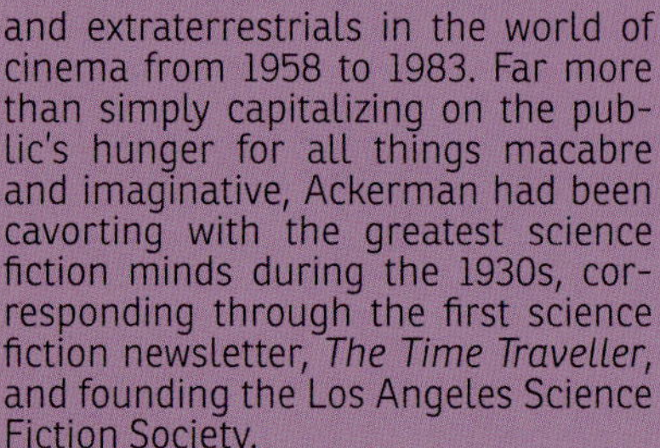

and extraterrestrials in the world of cinema from 1958 to 1983. Far more than simply capitalizing on the public's hunger for all things macabre and imaginative, Ackerman had been cavorting with the greatest science fiction minds during the 1930s, corresponding through the first science fiction newsletter, *The Time Traveller*, and founding the Los Angeles Science Fiction Society.

Ackerman and this small circle of social outcasts found in the futuristic pulp stories of the Great Depression Era a deep psychological link to society's dreams and fears. Forry could be seen throughout the 1930s and '40s walking around L.A. and New York City sporting a broad-shouldered spaceman's vest and long black cape, with zoot suit pants tucked into knee-length black leather boots and the symbol "4sJ" stitched across the center of the outfit's breastplate.

More than merely Shonberg's agent, Ackerman was something of a kindred spirit. He got Shonberg commercial art gigs creating cover images for a host of pulp sci-fi magazines (including several for *Famous Monsters of Filmland*). In his 1997 book, *Forrest J. Ackerman's World of Science Fiction*, Forry opens the book with a full chapter on the Frankenstein monster, calling Mary Shelley's 1818 *Frankenstein* novel (with its subtitle, *The Modern Prometheus*) the first work of science fiction. Inspired by German ghost stories that Shelly and her friends had been reading throughout the unusually wet summer of 1816, the novel galvanized the literary world in its time and has since been regarded as an international classic of gothic literature. However, Ackerman's interest wasn't limited to "serious" literature. To the contrary, he felt that the throwaway, the gregarious, the exploitative and the comically low-brow were equally important in understanding the myths of the modern world.

In the post-War environment of Los Angeles, jazz and cinema were more

popular than ever. An exodus of European modernists such as Fritz Lang, Bertolt Brecht, Kurt Weill, Marlene Dietrich and Thomas Mann escaped Nazi Germany by taking exile in L.A. during the period in which influential writers from the Roaring Twenties such as William Faulkner, Dorothy Parker, Nathanael West and F. Scott Fitzgerald had all moved to Hollywood to work as screenwriters. European radicals such as Christopher Isherwood, Anaïs Nin, Simone de Beauvoir, Gerald Heard and Aldous Huxley came to L.A., as well, Huxley and Heard becoming obsessed with the city's growing occultist practices and new hallucinogenic drugs. Along with scientist Jack Parsons, avant-garde filmmaker Kenneth Anger and pulp sci-fi novelist L. Ron Hubbard, Huxley and Heard envisioned a world on the brink of destruction, employing an expressionist language of technological speed, Babylonian excess, satanic reference and overt homosexuality that both appalled and intrigued the alienated youth of the post-War generation. Theirs was a generally more bleak vision of the future than that of Forry Ackerman and his science fiction collaborators.

Yet this is the world into which both Burt Shonberg and George Clayton Johnson entered upon arriving in Los Angeles in during the mid-1950s.

Before opening the Café Frankenstein, Johnson, like Shonberg, enlisted in the Army. He went to Auburn University on the G.I. Bill to study art too, but left by 1956 to travel around the U.S. In Los Angeles, Johnson met science fiction writers such as Theodore Sturgeon, Richard Matheson, Ray Bradbury and Forry Ackerman, who eventually introduced him to Rod Serling, producer of *The Twilight Zone*, and of course, Burt Shonberg.

By the time Johnson and Shonberg became fast friends, Shonberg was already living in two worlds: That of the commercial artist and, more provocatively, that of experimental bohemian. Johnson was acquainted with the works of Huxley, Heard and Anger by the mid-'50s, but didn't know them personally, nor does he recall if Shonberg knew these gentlemen or not. Shonberg did, however, become romantic with Jack Parsons's widow, Cameron (Marjorie Cameron Parsons Kimmel), a follower of the esoteric mystic Aleister Crowley and an accomplished painter in her own right. In 1957, Shonberg had what he referred to as his first "dramatic experience beyond the limits of so-called ordinary, everyday consciousness."

"Since this time," wrote Shonberg in his unpublished book *Out Here*, "via various methods, I have experienced a considerable number of altered states of consciousness. Among the methods employed to accomplish this was the use of what are termed psychedelic (mind-manifesting) substances. In 1960 I worked with a research project under the direction of a Los Angeles psychiatrist, Dr. Oscar Janiger, who was studying the effects of LSD-25 on the creative process. My participation in the project was that I had to do paintings under the influence of LSD-25."

These extraordinary paintings portray Shonberg sitting alone in a room with only a chair and a tape recorder. Suddenly, the atmosphere around him becomes alive with physical manifestations, culminating in the room splitting wide open and his conscious thoughts co-mingling with an illuminated outside environment. Whatever elements Shonberg may have

derived from surrealism and abstract expressionism up to this point, the drawings from *Out Here* signal the complete arrival at a mature style of his own.

"I was not in the City," Shonberg concluded in *Out Here*. "There was no city. I was not in the World. There was no world. I was right where I was, at that location, on the outer surface of the earth. I knew exactly where I was. I could see it. I was Here in Existence, and fully conscious of it."

"Burt loved LSD," confirmed Ledru Baker Shoopman, who died in 2007 in the same apartment that he and Shonberg roomed in together. "We both loved it. We took lots of acid. We painted things, intensely personal things. When I look at some of the canvases we did, I am still astonished by what I see. They go places most people would be afraid of."

"In the Los Angeles area," remembers poet Elizabeth Case, "it was called the Beat Generation. In San Francisco, they were called beatniks. Different terminology. The Los Angeles scene was dark and shadowy and more moody." In 1959, Shonberg created artwork for Case's anti-war poetry book, *Pax and Dig*, which was later recorded for an album in the late 1960s: Side one featuring the "Pax" poems narrated to the 3rd movement of Brahms' *Concerto in D-Flat Minor*, the "Dig" side backed by psychedelic rock and the cover art again done by Shonberg. In one of the book's more poignant drawings, the poem "Small Girl on Rubble" features Shonberg's rhythmic sense of draftsmanship in its most

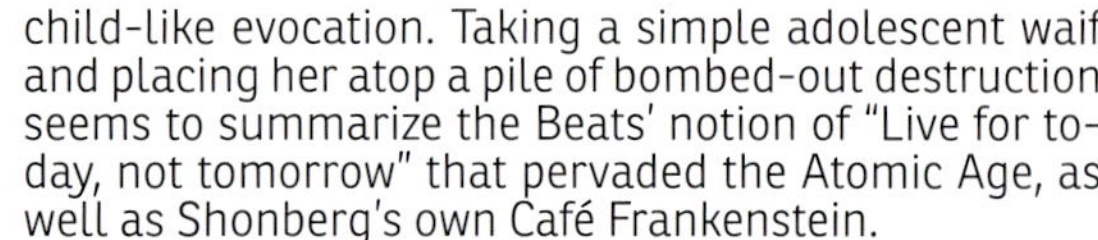

child-like evocation. Taking a simple adolescent waif and placing her atop a pile of bombed-out destruction seems to summarize the Beats' notion of "Live for today, not tomorrow" that pervaded the Atomic Age, as well as Shonberg's own Café Frankenstein.

"What I remember about the Frankenstein," said artist Leonard Kaplan, who died in 2008, "was the taboo that the community of Laguna felt about it." Kaplan, who lived behind Café Frankenstein during and after the coffeehouse's existence, was no stranger to controversy.

An intensely private man, Kaplan was a dealer in Pre-Renaissance art and a painter of haunted and erotic canvases that mixed the traditional world of oils with elements of taxidermy to create portraits of psychological terror, doubt, lust and violence. It is little surprise that Kaplan's work was only assessed after his death (an exhibit was held at the Laguna Art Museum in 2009), but not surprising at all that he was associated with the Café Frankenstein.

"At first," Kaplan related, "I thought these guys were a bunch of hucksters, ballyhoo and all. They were into jazz, I liked classical. But despite Laguna Beach being a supposed 'artists town,' I sensed in those guys a genuine outsider spirit."

Kaplan wasn't alone. In fact, the Frankenstein became a literal mecca for area artists whose work was on the fringes.

(top left) "To Be Is the Answer" - painting by Burt Shonberg, circa 1961. (Courtesy of Marshall Berle).

(above) "Psychedelic Art: A Group Exhibition" poster from 1965 with art by Shonberg. (Courtesy of Marshall Berle).

(bottom left) "Out Here" - painting by Burt Shonberg, circa 1965. (Courtesy of Marshall Berle).

(opposite) Frankenstein monster playing chess - wall mural by Shonberg. (Courtesy of George Clayton Johnson).

Don Karwellis, who later became head of the art department at the University of California Fullerton, created Toulouse-Lautrec style paintings of the Café Frankenstein scene. Tom Holste, whose later works were hung at the Guggenheim Museum in NYC, cut his teeth early on at the Frankenstein, painting airbrush portraits and abstracts on stretched canvas.

"Laguna Beach had a number of artists at that time," remembers Lewis Baltz, an important figure in the New Topographic movement of the late 1970s, who was a regular at the Frankenstein during his teenage years. "[These were] overwhelmingly seascape painters whose work seemed destined for furniture stores. There was also a very small group of 'serious' abstract painters. They were counter-culture *avant le mot*, but not exactly beatniks."

"The only artist who *looked* like a beatnik," continues Baltz, "was Andy Wing, a tall, gentle and shaggy man whose skein-like paintings showed a distinct influence of Pollock."

Many of Andrew Wing's murals can still be seen all over Laguna Beach today. Besides painting abstracts and making collages at Café Frankenstein, Wing turned his own Laguna Beach home into a folk environment of assemblage art in a similar style to Albert Glade's Enchanted Garden (1927-35) in Chino, CA, Simon Rodia's Watts Towers (1921-54) in South Central Los Angeles and Grandma Prisby's Bottle Village (1956-81) in Simi Valley. To this day, Wing's house, with its strewn pieces of colored glass, walkways of assembled broken pottery and strange collage paneling, sits back amongst tall-growing weeds along a back street just off the beach. Inside, a TV is constantly running, but no one ever answers the door.

Besides its collective of regularly-attending artists, the Café Frankenstein also boasted its share of quality bohemian music.

Irishman Michael Gaffney, who Baltz describes as "a petty thief and small-time drug dealer who had been in and out of jails since he was old enough to steal," played a particular brand of acoustic blues inside the Frankenstein.

"It depends on what your definition of performance was," says John Merrill, who played guitar in a psychedelic rock group dubbed the Peanut Butter Conspiracy from 1966-69. "I mean, the place was so small there wasn't even a stage. People would just sit on couches or sing from the corner of the room, real loose and all."

Other musical artists who played Café Frankenstein include future surf instrumental giant Dave Myers, folk chanteuse Judy Henske (who dated Woody Allen during the early '60s and inspired Allen's *Annie Hall* character) and Lee Mallory, a runaway from the Inland Empire who later became guitarist of the psych-pop act, the Millennium. Steve Gillette, who placed two songs on the first Linda Ronstadt/Stone Poneys album (and played guitar on the second), wrote of Café Frankenstein in the liner notes to his 1967 solo album:

"It was while I was working at the doughnut shop (the hours were 3 a.m. to 10 a.m.) and living in Whittier, California, that I used to drive down to a little coffee house -- now defunct -- at Laguna Beach to listen to folk music."

At other times, jazz guitarist Johnny Saint and flamenco guitarists such as Lenin Castro and a young Jose Feliciano played at the Frankenstein. "We also had a black conga drummer named Bob Collins," remembers Michael Schley, "and this guy named Philipo, who walked around with a typewriter and would type a bio or personality sketch for a buck." Philipo was actually Jack Phillips, a would-be TV personality who also called himself "John San Felipe."

But more often than not, it was Doug Myres, co-owner of the Frankenstein, who provided the entertainment.

By the time Café Frankenstein opened in 1958, Myres had already been a member of the Gateway Singers, a racially-integrated folk group who in 1952 were investigated by the House Un-American Activities Committee (HUAC), alongside New York City's the Weavers (featuring Pete Seeger), both bands accused of communist sympathizing (both cases later dismissed). After that, Myres became rhythm guitarist for the Easy Riders (featuring Terry Gilkyson, who wrote the huge-selling folk hit, "Marianne"), before opening the Frankenstein, where he would show up for performances in a hearse.

"It was a way-station between insanity and sanity," says Michael Schley, "a portal of life that people passed through. It was supposed to close at 4 a.m., but it rarely did. Burt and Doug also didn't shy away from controversy. To the contrary, they invited it."

From the outset, Café Frankenstein seemed to be a target for local police scrutiny. In an article titled

"The Café Espresso Kick," the June 1959 issue of *Rogue* magazine declared: "The local ladies' church league later complained of the use of stained glass in such a macabre undertaking, but withdrew their objections hastily when Frankenstein's owner threatened to erect a full-size cross bearing the unhappy monster." That incident merely scratched the surface.

On March 10, 1959, Laguna police hauled George Clayton Johnson, model Freda Kellogg and photographer Ron Vogel off to jail after receiving a tip that a group of kids saw Kellogg posing nude and playing bongos against the coffeehouse's interior mural artwork. The kids had apparently been peeking through the window cracks and reported their guffaws to local law officers, who also seized the photography negatives (which were later used in *Escapade* magazine's December 1959 issue). Said Judge C.C. Cravath at the trio's hearing (bearing indecent exposure, exhibitions and willful and lewd actions) on Tuesday April 14th: "I see a willful act, but don't see anything lewd involved." Case dismissed.

"That wasn't the first time we'd gone to court," insisted Sid Soffer, Café Frankenstein's manager from 1958 to the summer of '59, who passed away in 2008. "I got arrested for supposedly selling alcoholic beverages without a liquor license."

According to reports in the *Laguna Beach Post* dated June 26, 1958, Judge Cravath also heard this case. "Basically, I was putting a little brandy extract in the Cappuccino Royal," recalled Soffer. "It was so little that the alcohol pretty much evaporated when it was steamed. They tested it and everything in the courtroom."

The case, again, was dismissed. "They were out to get us from day one," insisted Soffer. "We didn't stand a chance."

Despite not being a co-owner, Sid Soffer was there from the outset. As part of the Laguna Carpentry Company, Soffer helped build the structure. Once he came to manage Café Frankenstein, Soffer cut a wall out on the south side of the coffeehouse and built a doorway for the patio. "I was the cook too," Soffer remembered fondly. "We served sandwiches, Italian water ices, French pastries from the Sarno Bakery in Hollywood, Dutch pastries from Almondas, lots of great little bistro items."

A few months after the nudity case, the Frankenstein again saw trouble. The Laguna Beach Board of Supervisors declared the coffeehouse outside of the defined entertainment zone, thus rebuking their license to allow live music (accepting only solo piano or organ).

"I got them to allow one instrument," said Soffer regarding the ordinance. "That was my last contribution to the café. It was passed that only piano and organ were allowed, but by getting it to be any one instrument, we could keep folk singers and bongo drums going."

By the end of the summer of 1959, Soffer left Café Frankenstein to start his own coffeehouse, the Blue Beet, at 460 S. Coast Boulevard in Laguna Beach. By 1960, Soffer moved his café out of Laguna, up to the nearby town of Newport Beach, where Sid's Blue Beet still operates near the Newport Pier to this day.

With the 1950s coming to a close, so too came the time for Johnson, Myres and Shonberg to be moving on. The trio sold Café Frankenstein to Michael Schley, who by that time was married to Constance Vining.

Vining had been running a sandal shop behind the Frankenstein (at 866 S. Coast Boulevard). Designs in Leather opened first in 1952 out of Vining's home in the Treasure Island Trailer Court, but moved into the Frankenstein building in 1958 and featured Shonberg mural art, as well.

Whatever attempts Laguna had made to kill off the monster, by the end of 1959, the town's youth was swept up in a more innocuous version of the bohemian phenomena. On December 10, 1959, the sophomore class at Laguna High School collectively decided to have a "beatnik day," sporting berets and sunglasses with black turtlenecks for the guys and black leotards for the girls. The *Laguna Beach Post* was again there to capture the moment with a front page snap. In early 1960, even the Laguna Playhouse was putting on John Osborne's disaffected play, *Look Back in Anger*, with its announced cast of "angry young men."

From 1960 to 1962, Michael Schley and Connie Vining ran Café Frankenstein simply as the 860 Club. "We lasted for a little while," laments Schley. "But once Shonberg was gone, everything that made the place unique went with it." Asked why that was, Schley suggests several reasons: "For one, Shonberg kept it edgy. But, you see, he was getting movie work and commercial work in Hollywood. With the way the town of Laguna was harassing him, you could hardly blame him for leaving."

After the 860 Club closed in 1962, Vining's Designs in Leather continued. But by 1964, both were gone, the building then razed and turned into a parking lot.

Schley moved up to Hollywood and ran the Xanadu Coffeehouse on Melrose Avenue, near Los Angeles City College, itself the stuff of legend (but that's another story).

As for George Clayton Johnson, he began writing for Rod Serling's *Twilight Zone* (eight episodes in all), as well the original Rat Pack vehicle, *Ocean's Eleven* (1960), the first episode of *Star Trek* (1966) and the classic science fiction novel, *Logan's Run*, which became an MGM film in 1976.

Burt Shonberg, by far the most interesting of the artists surrounding Café Frankenstein, continued creating commercial illustrations, mural commissions and fine art during the early 1960s.

His album artwork for Ron Goodwin's space-age bachelor pad LP, *Music in Orbit* (1958), features an Oz-like craft whose physiology combines a floating balloon apparatus with attached woodwind instruments and preternatural symbols, operating like a steam era piece of machinery. Childlike and esoteric at once, Shonberg's imaginative genius saw its full consummation of influences in one fell swoop: Outer-space, inner-mysticism and bohemian abstraction.

His portrait of Pyotr Tchaikovsky (used on the cover of Capitol Records' 1960 *Pathetique, 6th Symphony*) seems emblematic of Shonberg's style from 1960-62. Melding 18th Century impressionism with hints of cubism, the canvas becomes all Shonberg with the use of three dimensional splashes of color and symbolic imagery bursting from the Russian composer's head like living spirits of creativity. The burgundy, mustard yellow, black and powder blue

(opposite page) Burt Shonberg and Dave Myres inside Café Frankenstein from *Le Petit Sphinx #5*, 1959.

(top right) Freda Kellog at Café Frankenstein from *Escapade* magazine, December, 1959.

(right) More Shonberg mural work, from the interior wall at The Bastille. Photo from *Le Petit Sphinx #5*.

(below) Illustration from the *Music in Orbit* LP. (Courtesy of Ian Alloway).

hues were shades that Shonberg utilized heavily during this period, also creating a haunting portrait of Jesus Christ, who in the hands of Shonberg looks like a deeply tormented humanoid, his bald cranium enlargened and hallowed-out eye sockets speaking a kind of expressionistic terror.

Shonberg also created similar portraits for the 1960 film, *The Premature Burial*, and, most famously, for Roger Corman's American International Pictures film of *House of Usher*, also from 1960.

Shonberg's Usher paintings live and breathe horror, like everything in the house, the results for its characters being catastrophic. Shonberg also created a grand canvas titled "Premature Burial" for the 1960 film of the same name. The painting views like a complex rendering of Hell as described in Dante's *Inferno*. Previously, Shonberg had been the art director on such B films as *Code of Silence* (1957) and *The Brain Eaters* (1958).

He'd also kept busy creating murals for other coffeehouses and bohemian emporiums throughout the Greater Los Angeles area. Among these were: Cosmo Alley in Downtown Hollywood, Sandalsville on Fairfax Avenue, the Seven Chefs and the Bastille (both in West Hollywood), the Purple Onion on the Sunset Strip and the 40 Thieves Café in Venice Beach.

In 1963, Shonberg moved to Paris with Valerie Porter, who introduced him to Pablo Picasso. From Paris, the three of them (not necessarily together) went on to Ibiza in Spain, where Shonberg was also introduced to Dali by Porter. Shonberg returned to the U.S. in 1965 and settled for a while in Greenwich Village, where he took part in a group art show titled "Psychedelic Art" at the Coda Gallery in the nearby East Village. By year's end, Shonberg was back in Southern California.

Only four commercial pieces of art by Shonberg are known post-1963. One is a silly advertisement for filmmaker Don Brown's *Surfhouse*, a teenage surf movie theater, featuring a surfin' woodie printed with

(opposite top) Purple Onion mural by Shonberg, circa, 1962. (Courtesy of Ledru Baker Shoopman III).

(opposite left) Shonberg painting a mural at The Purple Onion. (Courtesy of Ledru Baker Shoopman III).

(opposite center) Sandalsville ad by Shonberg.

(top)"Premature Burial" painting by Shonberg from *House of Usher*. (Courtesy of Robert Skotek).

(center) Vincent Price with Shonberg painting from *House of Usher*. (Courtesy of Justin Humphreys).

(bottom) Shonberg (left) holds up one of his *House of Usher* paintings with Vincent Price. (Courtesy of Justin Humphreys).

Shonberg's inimitable mystic symbols all over. The second is the cover to Arthur Lee and Love's 1969 album, *Out Here*, which is really just a gatefold of Shonberg's 1965 painting of the same name. The piece portrays a human figure sitting at the edge of a hill, off in the horizon the sky opens up to him, striking a symbiotic relationship between the figure, the earth and the sky that is nothing short of hypnotic.

Then there was an album cover for the Curtis Brothers' self-titled debut on Polydor Records (1976), which utilized Shonberg's 1965 painting titled "Seated Figure and a Cosmic Train," which is described by Shonberg's friend Marhsall Berle as "a self-portrait of Burt Shonberg sitting in his living room in Laurel Canyon during an LSD experience."

Finally, Shonberg created artwork for Spirit's *The Spirit of 76 – Tampa Jam – Electro Jam from the Time Coast* album, based around a friendship that had blossomed between Shonberg and Spirit guitarist, Randy California.

All throughout the 1960s and '70s, Shonberg created wildly psychedelic and harrowingly spiritual artworks on canvas, wooden boards, music notation paper, napkins and just about any surface he could find. Sadly, very little of Shonberg's art has been exhibited as of this writing, though those who own Shonberg's artwork hold onto it dearly.

Marshall Berle has attempted to create a Burt Shonberg museum, but thus far has just gotten a web site off the ground. Ledru Baker Shoopman retained Shonberg's personal portfolio which contained hundreds of sketches and personal clues about Burt's life. However, since Shoopman's passing in 2007, his long-time girlfriend Joie has not returned phone calls.

Shonberg did have one retrospective during his lifetime. Inside his portfolio was a poster for a 1967 Shonberg exhibition (sponsored by Gary Grief) at the Gallery Contemporary at 631 N. La Cienega Boulevard, the central arts district of L.A.

Burt Shonberg died on September 16, 1977. His artwork has never been exhibited in a museum setting. Like much painting and sculpture from the 1960s, Shonberg is yet to receive his full curatorial due for the unique vision he portrayed on canvas.

Yet one thing that rings true of both Café Frankenstein and Burt Shonberg is their overwhelming sense of secular humanism that, for a brief period in the late 1950s, teemed with imagination and controversy: A largely unknown domain waiting to be re-discovered by historians and lovers of the Beat Generation.

Quoted excerpts from the book *Out Here* have been reprinted by permission of the copyright owner at www.burtshonberg.com.

On October 19-21, 2012, the San Diego Comic Fest is staging a re-construction of the Café Frankenstein with the original coffeehouse's owner, George Clayton Johnson, serving as Storyteller in Residence and re-creations of Burt Shonberg's stained-glass windows by artist Wendy All.

Four Eyed Figures

by Charles Schneider

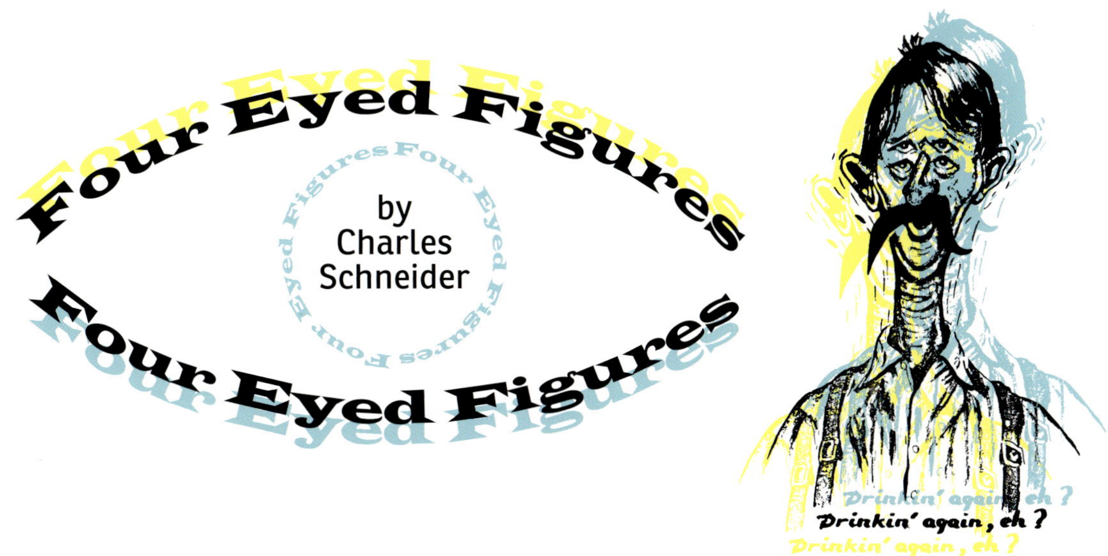

I picked up my first four-eyed figure at the Park West Antiques Fair in Chicago, Illinois sometime in the early 1970s. This would begin a life-long fascination and quest for other images and objects containing this reoccurring theme – a man, or a woman, with four-eyes. My first find took the shape of a clever novelty ashtray, beautifully sculpted and cast in a thin lead-like metal. It is an ashtray that features two trays for cigarettes, which, once inserted, fill the hollow interior with smoke. Holes in the ears and mouth allow the smoke to slowly escape. An example of this ashtray, cast in metal, can be seen on the following page.

The origin of the image has not been determined, but the secret meaning behind it is clear. The four-eyed image suggests drunkenness and intense, unrepentant intoxication. What makes it unique is the fact that WE, the observer, are viewing the drunk, as he sees us – as a blurred double vision. This clever flip-flop of consciousness oddly has the ability to make the viewer feel dizzy himself, and disoriented, even nauseated. Thus, several incredible examples of the four-eyed character have "normal" two-eyes on one side. In the course of a festive night, the owner was supposed to slyly turn the figure around – making an already soused pal think that they were, indeed, "seeing double." Two fine examples of the man and the woman are shown on the next spread of the article.

The image reoccurs throughout pop culture history. Both *MAD* Magazine's beloved Alfred E. Newman, as well as *Cracked* magazine's sleazy mascot Sylvester P. Smythe have sported four-eyes on their magazine covers. No less an artist than Man Ray took an indelible and hallucinatory photograph of the magnificent femme fatale Countess Casati, in which he brilliantly branded her with four-eyes. Early German expressionist cinema also abounds in this image. The rock band Pink Floyd featured a classic four-eyed bottle opener on the cover of their album *Relics*, with an actual human tongue protruding from it. Bleggh!

Because the four-eyed image is so clearly connected with an altered state of consciousness, it is often found in the form of booze bottles, drinking mugs and so forth. A very special bottle (see photo on the last page of the article) depicts an embracing set of four-eyed drunks, respectively named "Scotch" and "Rye." The famed Magic Castle, in Hollywood, has two very rare variations, in framed engraving form, on either side of the legendary first floor bar. It may also be found on a myriad of common objects ranging from decals, postcards, posters, wooden plaques, lighters and even salt and pepper shakers. One charming pair consists of a couple in a barrel, designed to gently rock within, before going over the falls! Once you start looking for them, it seems the world is filled with four-eyes. I'll drink to that! HiCCC!

(this page – top) KWITCHERBELLYAKIN decanter
(center) Four-eyed ceramic bottle stoppers
(bottom) Smoking ashtray in cast iron
(right) Four-eyed themed bar towel

(opposite page) Double-sided ceramic man and woman figures by Alexander Backer & Co.

Fancy another drink?

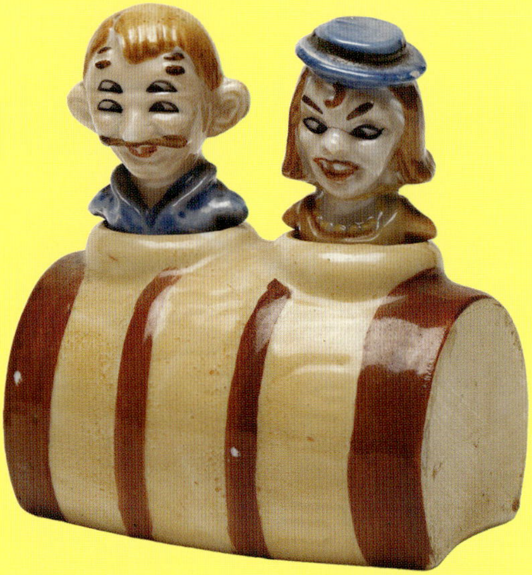

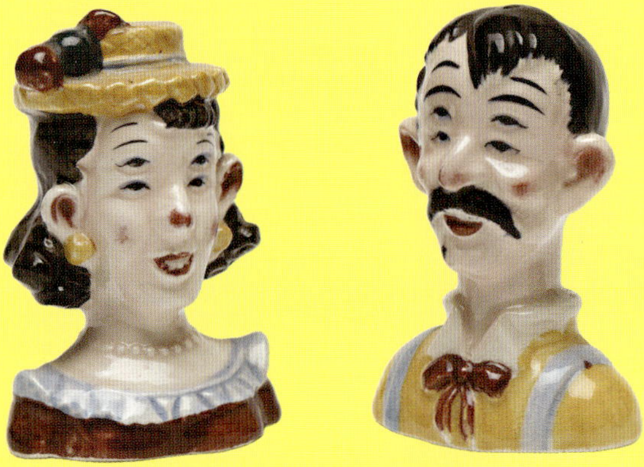

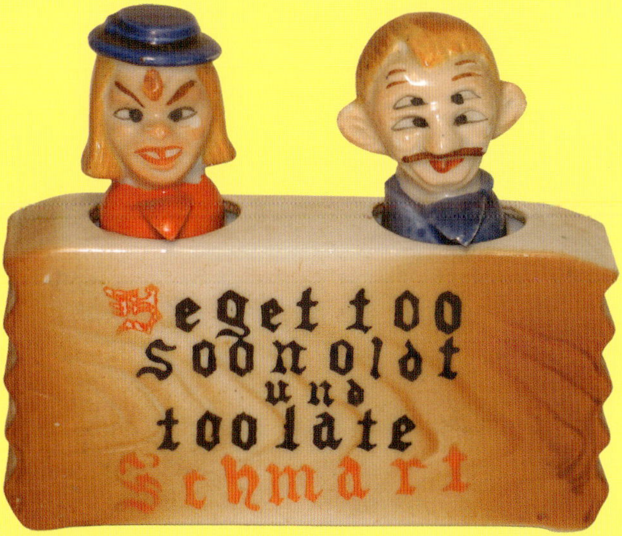

(opposite page – left column) three examples of four-eyed salt and pepper shakers. The top and bottom couple rock back and forth when tipped.

(opposite page – right column) three examples of the most common of four-eyed objects – the cast iron bottle opener.

(this page) At top, three examples of four-eyed decanters – two with a twist! One is actually a rare six-eyed figure, and the other a hard to find two headed four-eyed figure. At left is a four-eyed mug. To the right here is an ex-libris bookplate of author of this article – Charles Schneider by sci-fi artist Kelly Freas.

Murals of the Black House

Photographs by Nicholas Syracuse

Text by Martin McIntosh

Anton Szandor LaVey, author of *The Satanic Bible* and founder of The Church of Satan, lived in a residence with his family that became known over the years as The Black House. Situated on California Street in San Francisco's Richmond district, it served both as the headquarters of the Church of Satan which he formed in 1966 and also as LaVey's home until his death in 1997. The house itself stood out in stark contrast to the other surrounding Victorian buildings with its black painted exterior. LaVey decorated the residence incorporating his iconoclastic style to the interior. It was home to his astounding collections of the weird and wondrous including headstone coffee table, human skeleton, circus and sideshow posters,medieval weapons, and many other objet d'art and memento mori. Quite the scene, and to top it off a number of the walls of the house LaVey painted with particularly evocative murals.

One of LaVey's more personal and least documented pursuits was painting. There is one published photo (in his biography *The Secret Life of a Satanist*) of him standing in front of one of his paintings with an Addams Family-esque house in the background and a diabolical axe wielding figure in the foreground. One also occasionally glimpses paintings by LaVey in the background of publicity shots (numerous news wire photos spread the globe after the Church's founding in 1966): Beelzebub in flight is visible in one photo, a misty night scene in another. His paintings are featured in more detail in the two documentaries about LaVey - *Satanis* (1970) and *Speak of the Devil* (1995). Some of his paintings also appear in a 1965 episode of the innovative children's program *Brother Buzz* where The Black House is featured along with him and his pet lion Togare.

In *Satanis* LaVey describes his paintings as "nightmare visions". As the camera pans over some of the works, we see one depicting the silhouette of a vulture on a tombstone with a shimmering moon overhead. Next to that is a portrait of a grotesque looking veiled woman. Another has a skeleton on a roller coaster riding high in the air next to a mysterious tower and night sky. The exact whereabouts of these paintings today is not certain, but they are most likely in the private collections of his family and friends. So for now, the guardians of these paintings have the pleasure of viewing them all to themselves.

LaVey's paintings and murals have a wonderful enigmatic quality and evoke *Weird Tales* era artists such as Lee Brown Coye, and equally atmospheric painters like Joseph Mugnaini (most famous for his work on Ray Bradbury book covers). LaVey's artwork, particularly his paintings, are at once both grotesque and intriguing. He acknowledged other influences such as the techniques of painter Ivan Albright and photographer William Mortensen, whose book *The Command To Look* made a lasting impression on LaVey's understanding of composition and the compelling nature of certain aesthetic principles.

Filmmaker Kenneth Anger was a good friend and regular house guest of LaVey. In the 1950s Anger had journeyed to the home of Aleister Crowley, another famous figure of the occult, at the Abbey of Thelema in Cefalù, Italy and uncovered Crowley's murals. Whilst these painted walls remain to this day, LaVey's home and murals are no more.

New York based photographer Nicholas Syracuse was insightful enough to photograph the murals of The Black House for prosperity's sake. The photographs of four of the murals in the house which you see here were taken in August 1998.

The Black House was sadly demolished in 2001. In its place now sits an unremarkable and undistinguished duplex dwelling that might as well be in a generic strip anywhere in the increasingly characterless landscape of the 21st century.

Photograph of LaVey and acolytes taken in the Black House just months before he founded the Church of Satan.

This imposing mural was located in LaVey's kitchen near his array of keyboards where he played his music. The image was inspired by Chernabog from the "Night On Bald Mountain" scene in Disney's *Fantasia*. The name is Slavic for "black god". Here he sits atop a fiery mountain. For much of the mural's existence a Sigil of Baphomet plaque (the inverted pentagram and goat's head symbol of the Church of Satan), was positioned just below Chernabog's hands.

This winged creature, inspired by German artist Martin Schöngauer's engraving of "Temptation of St. Anthony", sits with its back to a window in the Black House's kitchen. This mural stands out proudly against the black of the wall. Just hinted at in the left of this photo the mural continues, to show other grotesque creatures.

Blank walls were the antithesis of the Black House. Even the bathroom didn't escape LaVey's artistry. Here an octopus looked over the bathtub. Peeling paint and cobwebs lend themselves to complement the otherworldly mood of this scene.

Here a pipe is incorporated into the mural image of a pitchfork wielding devil, perhaps piping him directly to the gates of Hell. The photograph once again captures the cobwebs which formed over time, contributing to the atmosphere one might expect in the house of the Addams Family, an analogy often used when describing LaVey and his family.

IL VITTORIALE DEGLI ITALIANI · FONDAZIONE

GABRIELE D'ANNUNZIO'S

IL VITTORIALE

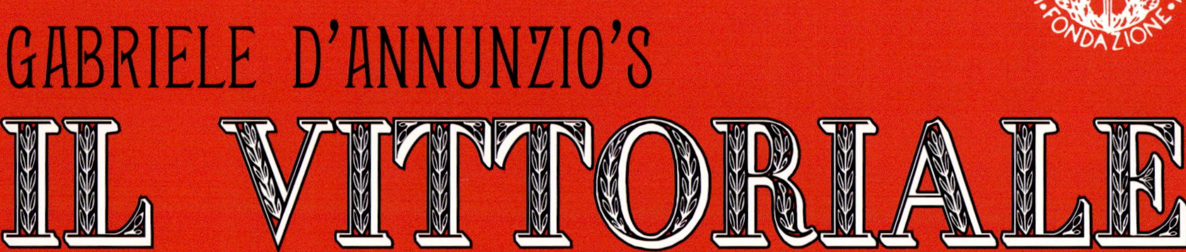

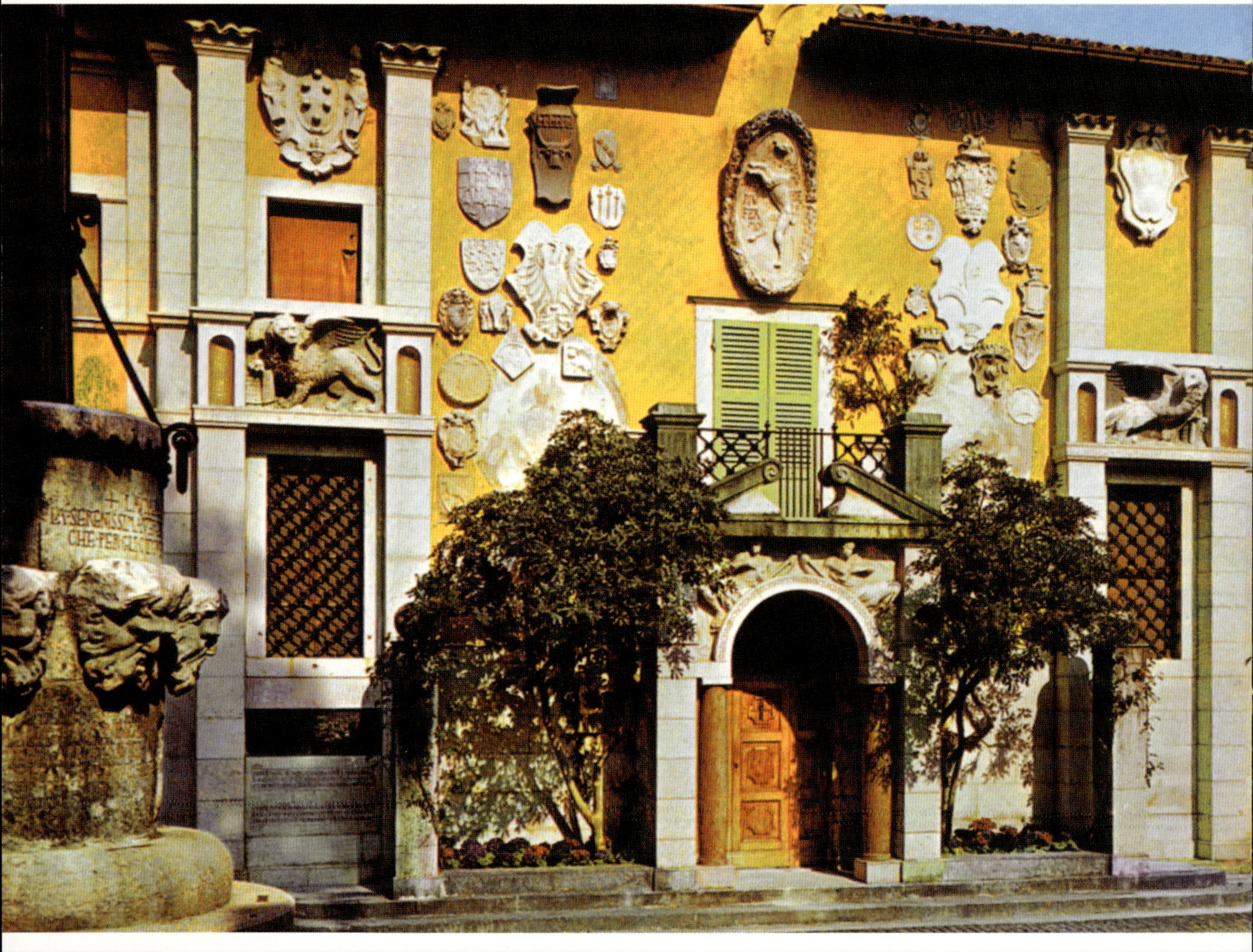

BY MARTIN McINTOSH

Gabriele d'Annunzio is one of those unique individuals who give true meaning to the term. His residence Villa Cargnacco is part of Il Vittoriale, a museum-like theme park honoring d'Annunzio that he himself, together with his personal architect Giancarlo Maroni, spent almost two decades designing and furnishing. D'Annunzio lived here from 1921 until his death in 1938. Il Vittoriale is so imbued with character that once visited one feels like having spent meaningful time with its creator, even if that person has been dead for over 70 years.

It was 2009, my wife and I were traveling around Italy and Germany. I was familiar with d'Annunzio and had read a little about Il Vittoriale, but our time in Italy was tight and we hadn't planned on going that far north. Whilst in Bologna I received an email from artist Charles Krafft (he of Delft Disasterware fame). After learning I was in Italy he implored we alter our plans and make a detour. Krafft's recommendation and subsequent encouragement, together with the realization we could indeed squeeze in a visit, was too much to pass up. A couple of days later at dawn we left our base in Bologna and took a train to Prescia and then bussed it to Gardone Riveria, the town where Il Vittoriale sits overlooking Lake Garda.

Fittingly, the estate proved to be as rich and complex as the man himself. D'Annunzio, often referred to as the warrior-poet, packed a lot into his 74 years and could be considered something of an overachiever in many facets of life. From an early age he excelled at poetry and writing (his first verse was published while still at school). His literary career was extensive and his works are celebrated for their power and decadence. He was a very active participant in World War I, fighting as a pilot and highly awarded as a military man. He gave numerous rousing public speeches gaining popularity amongst the Italian people for his orations and deeds. D'Annunzio's lovers were many and included (but certainly not limited to) actress Leonora Duse, and Marchesa Luisa Casati - the latter arguably 20th century Europe's most eccentric heiress, muse and patroness. His relationship with the famed Casati was a life long on-again, off-again affair that continued until just a few years before his death.

As well as being celebrated as a literary figure and for his glorious war involvement, d'Annunzio was also loved for his taking of Fiume with his own personal army for the Italian people. There he set up a proto-Fascist system with himself as dictator - Benito Mussolini would later "borrow" many of d'Annunzio's elements for his own Fascist movement. D'Annunzio's rule was quick yet momentous - a little over a year after taking it he surrendered Fiume back to the Italian state, and returned home. It was after this return that his personal secretary, Tom Antongini, located the perfect villa for him at Gardone Rivera, that would be transformed into Il Vittoriale.

Over the near twenty years of its design and construction there would be many elements added to the grounds. D'Annunzio had the *Puglia*, a battleship captured at Fiume, placed in the garden. An orchestra often played atop it, and guns would regularly be blasted in salute of important visiting guests. An amphitheatre, in the classic style, was built near the entrance of the property. Also on the grounds was a naval vessel d'Annunzio had captained, and the aeroplane he flew over Vienna during an infamous World War I pamphlet drop.

Whilst the entire property of Il Vittoriale was inspiring, it was the tour of d'Annunzio's personal residence that was the highlight for me. The week before we had visited King Ludwig's Neuschwanstein Castle in Bavaria, which is worth comparing to d'Annunzio's estate. Both destinations provided abundant evidence of each man's obsessions and excesses, but the tour of Ludwig's castle was superficial, crowded and rushed. In comparison, the visit of the poet's abode was intimate and well paced allowing time to savor the atmosphere. Even still I was compelled to take the tour of d'Annunzio's home again, and the second journey was even better than the first. Smaller details were further revealed and appreciated.

The residence itself is moderately large but not spacious nor grandiose. But it is lavish in its execution, and the interior is crammed with furniture, paintings, books and relics of every kind. Every surface it seems is covered - whether it be with an object, decoration, rug or fabric. Even the lavatory is decked out with a collection of masks from all around the globe. In the house, one's senses are overwhelmed. Many of the rooms are dark without direct sunlight and lit merely by indirect sources. The dim environment with its mood lighting is the

ideal setting for the many vivid objects and finishes - lustrous blues, crimson reds and rich wood tones - d'Annunzio preferred. The air also had a unique quality to it - not just the smell of old stuff, but something else, an almost magical quality, that I couldn't put my finger on. This is a residence unlike any other I have ever encountered.

When d'Annunzio first acquired the property the existing house was typically Teutonic having belonged to a German art historian, and rather nondescript. Speaking to his architect Maroni, d'Annunzio stated "I leave to you the skeleton of the construction, keeping the adornment for myself". And adorn he did. Towards this goal he received significant funds from Mussolini who was threatened by d'Annunzio's popularity amongst the Italian people. D'Annunzio also disagreed with the Fascists on a number of issues, and Mussolini was very keen to keep him out of the capital and occupied with the mammoth task of converting the estate in his obsessive and lavish manner.

He approached the design of his home the way that he would compose his poetry. The house is an artistic embodiment of the man. Conceived as a "book of living stones", a poem composed not of words, but highly symbolic ornamentation and displays. It's all best described in his own words: "In fact everything here has been created and transfigured by me. Everything here bears the imprint of my style ... My love of Italy, my cultivation of memories, my aspiration to heroism ... is manifested here in every search for line, in every accord or discord of color".

On the following pages, we present a photographic tour of some of the highlights from Il Vittoriale. And even if you don't come close by chance, I recommend going out of your way to visit. You won't regret it.

(previous page – left) The entrance of d'Annunzio's residence Villa Cargnacco.

(previous page – right) D'Annunzio dressed in a fine suit reading. He always presented himself in style.

(above) The prow of the ship *Puglia* with bronze figurehead of "Victory" at front by sculptor Renato Brozzi.

(right) An aerial view of Ill Vittoriale. At front is the Parlaggio, Il Vittoriale's large amphitheatre, center is D'Annunzio's residence Villa Cargnacco, and top the Mausoleum (constructed after d'Annunzio's death). To the right the mast of the *Puglia* breaks through the trees.

Inside Villa Cargnacco...

(above) The Globe Room - the name comes from the large globe on one of the tables. The walls are lined with bookshelves and house 6,000 books. There are 33,000 books total in all rooms combined. As with virtually all other rooms in the house, objets d'art decorate the setting together with fabrics, rugs and furniture. Generally all had very specific placement, meaning and significance to d'Annunzio. The house is a living work of art.

(left) The Zambracca - this is the first room of the bedroom wing. Zambracca is an old word meaning "the lady of the bed chamber". D'Annunzio died at the table here on the evening of March 1, 1938, of a brain hemorrhage. A wall plaque of Medusa is one of the many objects that can be seen here. At the desk, amongst the numerous items, is a silver eagle's head by sculptor Renato Brozzi. This is one of many other sculpted animals around the residence by Brozzi. Dominating the room is a cast of the head of Michelangelo's Dawn, which d'Annunzio himself gilded. Also in this room, is a cabinet of d'Annunzio's medicines (including laudanum) that he regularly consumed. He would often work through the night until the dawn. As he grew older, he regularly found it difficult to fall asleep and used various medicines to assist him with sleep.

SE·TV·VVOI·CHE·LA·TVA·CASA·TI·PAIA·GRANDISSIMA·PENSA·DEL·SEPOLCRO·
NIVNA·CASA·E·SI·PICCOLA·CHE·NON·

(opposite - top) Room of the Mutilated - this small book-lined room was planned to be a study. D'Annunzio received a huge amount of correspondence. As he could not, or did not want to, answer all of these letters, he said that he was mutilated and thus unable to write. The room is named from the relief above the entrance door of an amputated hand and the inscription that translates to "the amputee rests".

(opposite - bottom) The Blue Bathroom - this room alone features over 900 art objects including many aquatic animals. Numerous tiles with a myriad of motifs and patterns are also mounted on the walls.

(above) The Lepers Room - d'Annunzio would often retreat here to meditate. This room is perhaps the one in the entire residence that requires the most work to decipher all of the symbols and mottos within - including the paintings on the walls and ceiling. A bed is at center. It is a hybrid shape between a cradle and coffin, and like much of the decor is poetically symbolic and layered with esoteric significance. D'Annunzio wanted this to symbolize birth and death. After own death, he left strict instructions of how his body was to be laid out in this room.

(opposite) The Room of the Relics - the deep red of the ceiling and floor rugs complement d'Annunzio's collection of mementos and religious portraits. On a high ledge running along three of the walls are antique wooden statues of saints and angels. A pyramid of gods from Eastern religions are on one wall. Other objects populate the setting including an altar for a broken steering wheel out of a boat that Englishman Sir Henry Segrave was killed in while attempting to break a speed record. It was d'Annunzio who had suggested to him to make the speed attempt.

(above) The Workshop - this was d'Annunzio's main working room. The door of this room was made deliberately low so as one entering must lower their head to honor the work completed here. It is one of the brightest rooms of the house, and that is emphasized by the light oak that is used for all the furnishings. A covered bust of one of his lovers, Eleonora Duse, stands on one of the tables. D'Annunzio had a portrait by Man Ray of another of his lovers, Countess Casati, prominently displayed in here. The portrait remains in here to this day, amongst other select photographs.

(left) Room of the Cheli – here is d'Annunzio's art deco style dining room. This was the last room of the residence to have been decorated. The walls are brightly colored lacquered wood. Cheli was the name of a giant tortoise at the end of the table. It had died in d'Annunzio's garden from stomach poisoning. The shell is the original, and the body and head were sculpted in bronze by Renato Brozzi. The room is illuminated by large windows with geometric designs and made from polychrome alabastrine glass. The bronze faun and nymph to the right are by Pierre Le Faguays.

(below) D'Annunzio was an absolute aesthete. This is evident at every turn in Il Vittoriale - whether it be the residence, grounds, vehicles or personal effects of d'Annunzio. Here a red jacket of d'Annunzio's hangs beside an assortment of his boots.

TOLMER'S WORLD

Roger Tolmer (1908-1988) was an artist born in Sotteville-lès-Rouen, France, a small town in Seine-Maritime nestled very near Rouen, where Marcel Duchamp began his career and Joan of Arc ended hers.

At the end of the 1960s and beginning of the 1970s, the claim that 1% of all things art should be monumental had become a kind of official national motto in the France of de Gaulles, then Pompidou and Giscard. At that time, authorities believed in edifying the masses by the means of dynamic, enormous works of art.

Tolmer created 32 stratified, polyester structures. White, aubergine and clay colours adorned these space-age bas-reliefs.

In Philippe Priol's 1998 monograph on Tolmer, one could read about the journey that had begotten the resin structures: "the Sardaigne landscapes [are] defined by big, whitish, crystal-clear blocks, which are actually huge rocks that the passing of time and the bad weather have modeled into a variety of geometrical shapes with round, concave, convex or salient edges".

Tolmer's structures can be seen in Pierre Granier-Deferre's 1975 film *Adieu Poulet* (*The French Detective*) starring Lino Ventura and Patrick Dewaere. But do not think I'm wallowing in nostalgia here, since monumental art under Pompidou's and Giscard's regimes reflected a true belief in a brilliant future, in which the modern man would drive along the Autobahn in his DS car to eventually fly away on the Concorde, after having stopped over at Jacques Borel's full-flavoured restaurants (the ones you see in the film *L'Aile Ou La Cuisse*).

In 1969, the year Tolmer's sculptures were designed, Y2K was a mere sci-fi projection. One could only dream of a *Star Trek*-like world, full of aerodynamics, plastic and Plexiglass. Finally, once they had landed in 2000, the children who were born 30 years before had become disillusioned. More *Blade Runner* than *Star Trek*, the future was not what it used to be! Never mind ... what's more important is how current authorities tend to overshadow such patrimony. Space-age years have seemingly never existed, as if their elegant (though shaky) plans, their luxuriance and their naive faith in the future had no right to exist.

Just like Joe Stalin's friends have gradually disappeared from official photos, our 1% of monumental pop art has little by little given way under the blows of the demolition men. Pop forms and rhythms made of modern resin should show us the way to the brilliant future I was mentioning. But it's as if none of it happened. I was able to save four of Tolmer's sculptures before their programmed destruction; others had the good fortune of decorating the front of one of Sotteville's schools.

I have always dreamt of Tolmer's structures as Kubrickian monoliths rising into space emitting cosmic rays which would deliver us from our local consciousness into a more global one. No drugs are needed to see the characteristic lysergic tangles of Tolmer's work.

Who cares whether Tolmer is a minor or a major artist, or whether his paintings have limited merit? He worked at a time, the late 1960s, when the charm and modernity prevalent in the air gave talent to people whose interest as creators simply vanished afterwards.

For example, Jean-Claude Vannier, the wonderful arranger behind Gainsbourg's *Melody Nelson* album and countless mind-boggling late 1960s singles, as well as the composer of *L'Enfant Assassin Des Mouches*, has only created musical 'guano' since then. Tolmer's structures are of the same kind - they are recipients of LSD vibes, Jack Kirby, space-age pop, Michel Colombier, Jacques Rouxel, Jean-Christophe Averty or *Goodbye Vienna*.

That's the reason why some have destroyed that 1% at the beginning of the 2000s. It is our duty to refuse the pragmatic and sordid future awaiting us - peri-urban commercial zones, suburban air-conditioned look alike semis, a whole world living as a standardized province. Tolmer's structures are a link, a Chronos loop that one may use to redirect space and time. The future happened yesterday and it's up to us to create new aerodynamically-streamlined times.

MASKED

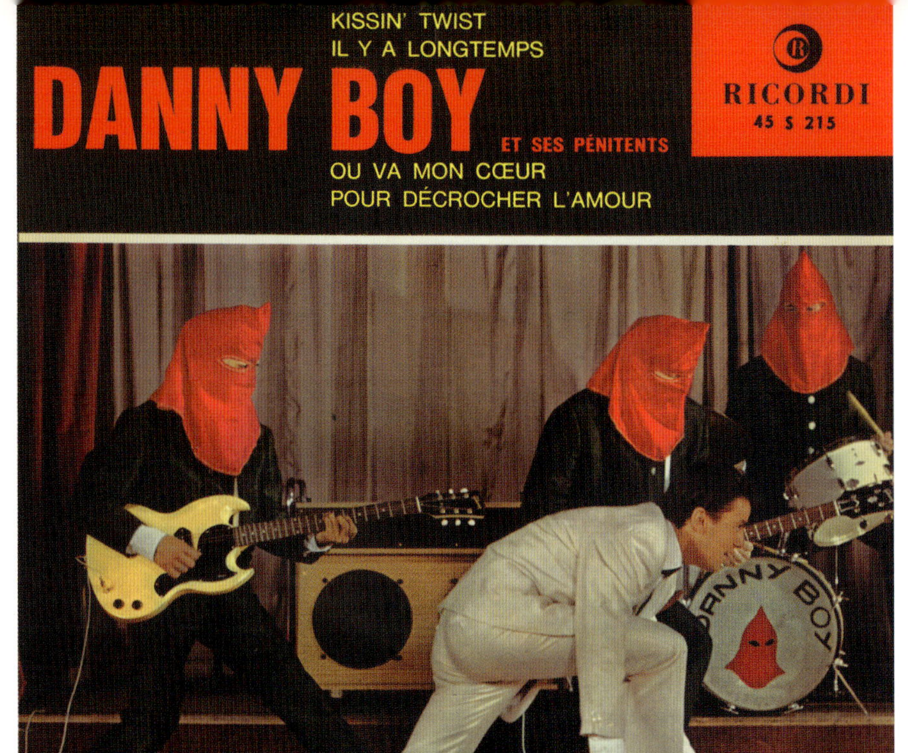
KISSIN' TWIST
IL Y A LONGTEMPS
DANNY BOY
ET SES PÉNITENTS
OU VA MON CŒUR
POUR DÉCROCHER L'AMOUR
RICORDI
45 S 215
DANNY BOY

DANNY BOY
ET SES PENITENTS
STOP! • HA! HA! • LE TWIST DE SCHUBERT
• LETTRE OUVERTE
TWIST

RICORDI
45 S 210

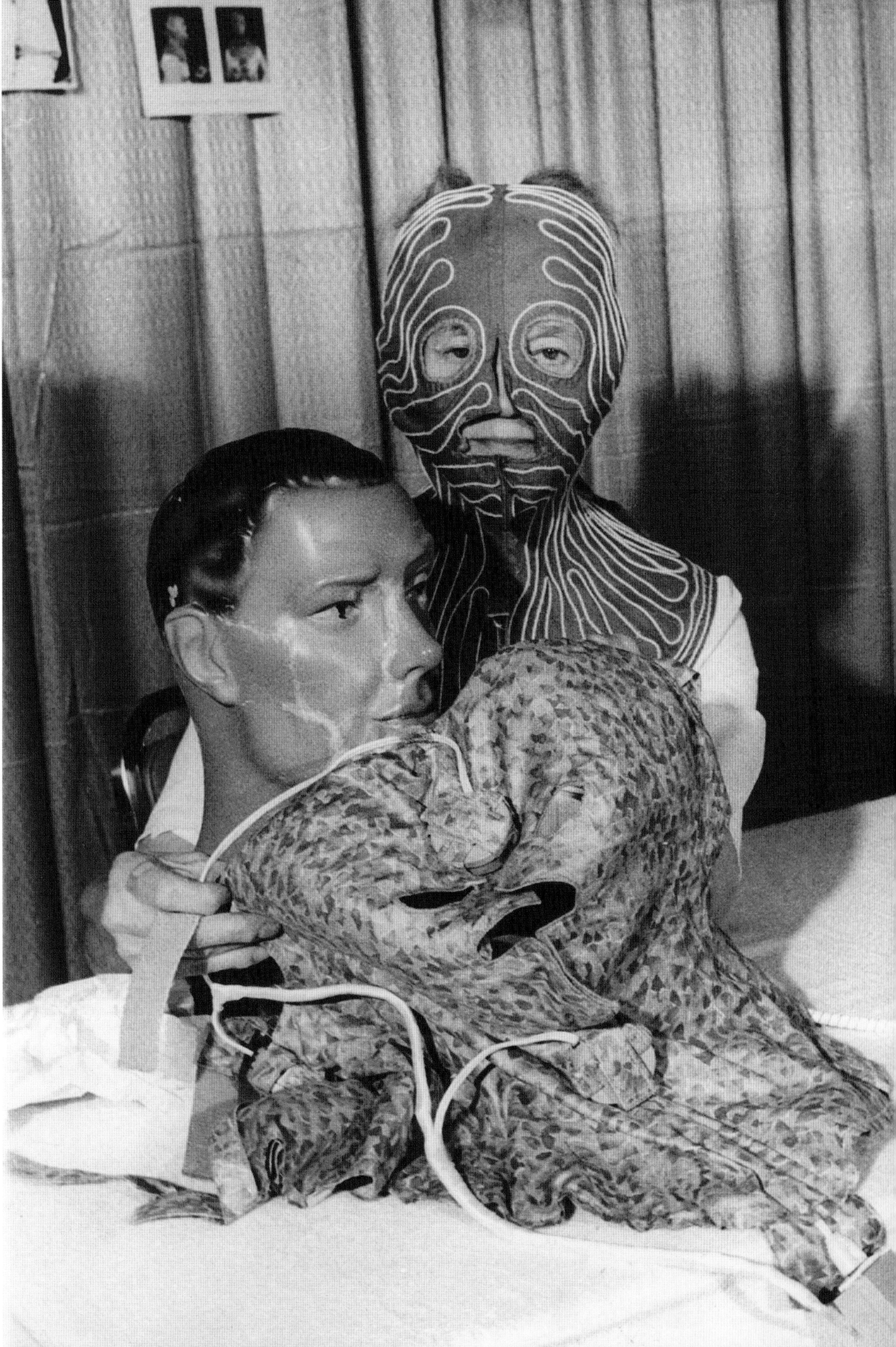

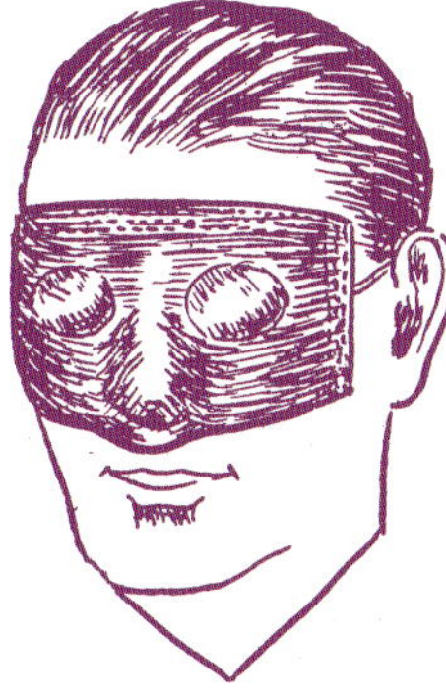

FIRST ALBUM
THE "YOU KNOW WHO" GROUP
THE BOYS WITH THAT GREAT NEW ENGLISH SOUND
THIS ALBUM INCLUDES:
ROSES ARE RED MY LOVE
HEY YOU AND THE WIND AND THE RAIN
IT'S A FUNNY THING (THAT MONEY CAN DO)
AUTUMN LEAVES
IT WAS ONLY YESTERDAY
HOW CAN SHE LIVE (WITHOUT ME)
BLUE IS THE NIGHT
REELIN AND ROCKIN
RED RIVER VALLEY
THIS DAY LOVE
TELL ME (HOW DO I SAY GOODBY?)
ALBERTA
INTERNATIONAL
MONO 1A420

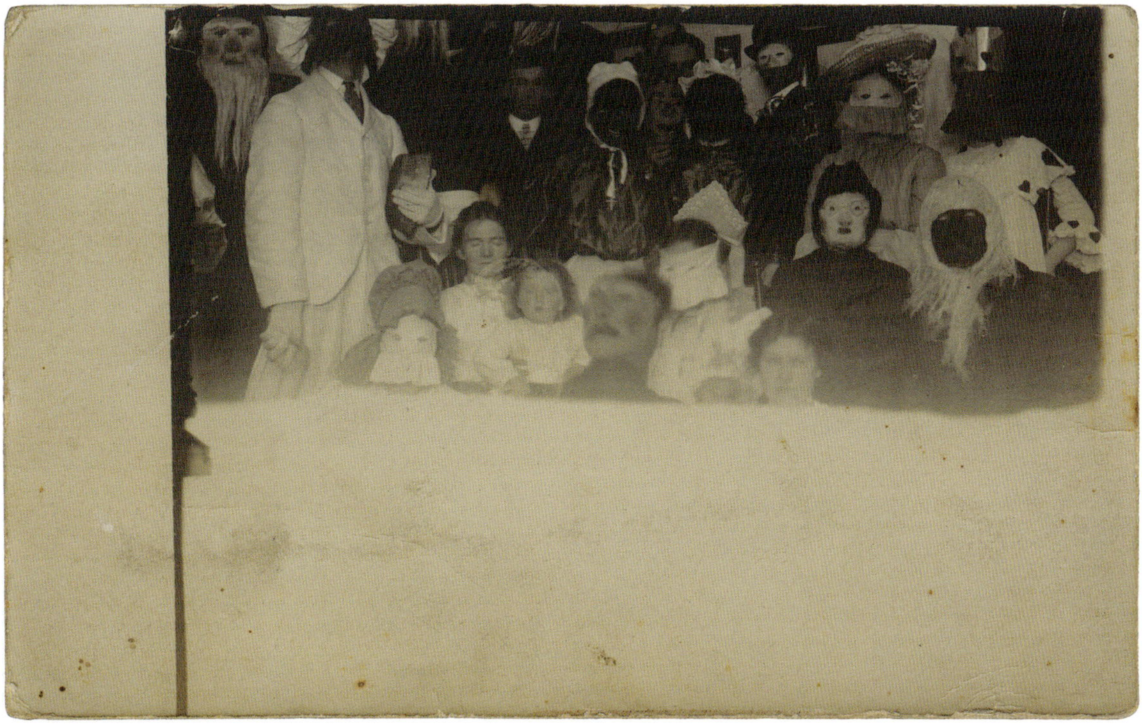

DRY
YOU WASH

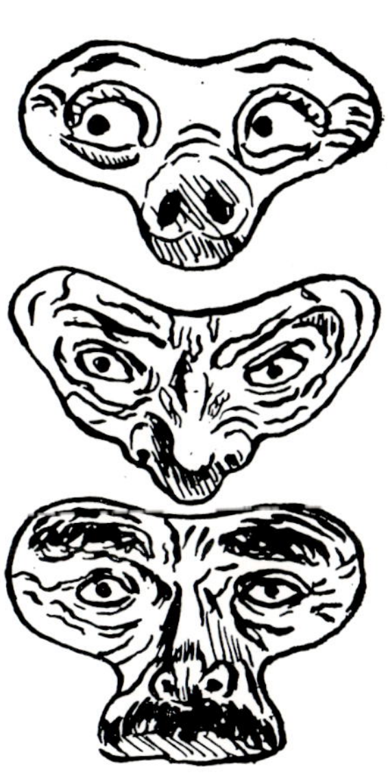

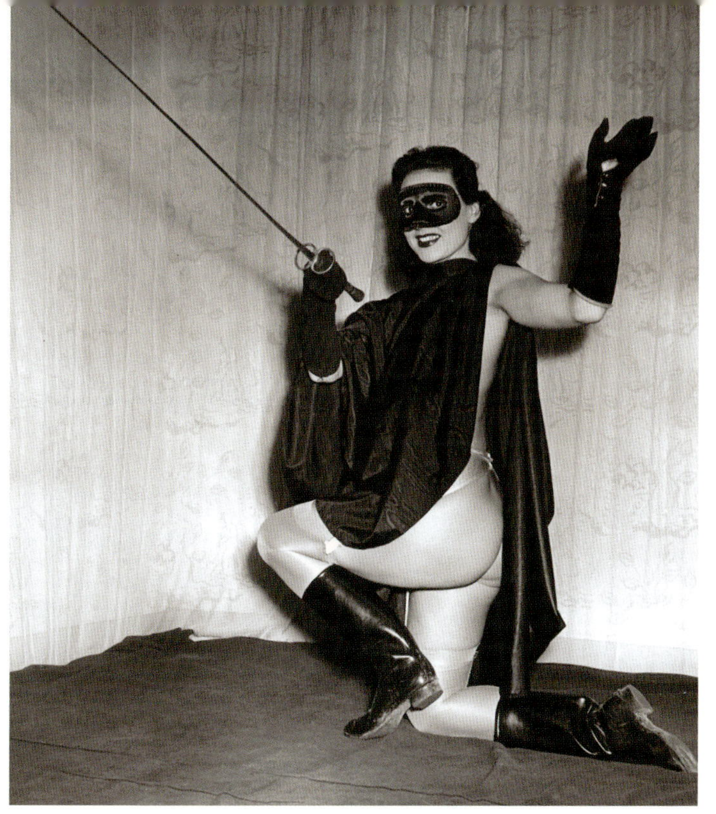

NOV • 69 •

MASKED MARVEL

JUL • 58

¢
Strange Mask
MADE IN HONG KONG

STEREO ... *also available in HIGH FIDELITY* DS-888

ART and DOTTY TODD

DART RECORDS

Black Velvet Eyes

ORCHESTRA CONDUCTED BY HENRI BEAU

THE SUBURBAN HEADHUNTER

the cult of ren clark, his polynesian village and the severed head mug

by martin mcintosh

On the grounds of the Western Hills Hotel in Fort Worth a peculiar establishment – Ren Clark's Polynesian Village could be found. One of the hundreds of Tiki themed bars and restaurants that existed in cities across America in the 1950s and 1960s, Ren Clark's Polynesian Village wasn't the biggest nor most elaborate. Nor was it in existence for long - it operated from 1960 until 1969 when it was reportedly destroyed by a fire. But, of an already rich and fascinating pedigree of Tiki bars to exist, it certainly was one of the most interesting. And that can be traced backed to its owner and namesake - Ren Clark and an odd little ceramic vessel of a severed head in which exotic cocktails were served.

Ren Clark was a magician. In 1940, long before his Polynesian Village was born (to borrow a quote from the restaurant's poetic menu) out of "fire and brimstone", Clark had formed the Fort Worth Magicians Club. He had found his fortune as a young man with an oil strike in Crosscut, Texas that enabled him to pursue his passions, the biggest of which was magic - both as a performer and collector. His enthusiasm was legendary. His home had its own magic stage where he hosted magical galas and gatherings. This enthusiasm it seems was carried through to Ren Clark's Polynesian Village. Here he both entertained and dined the cocktail set seeking a night of dining, drinking and entertainment.

Clark died in 1991, but it wasn't until 2009 that his estate was auctioned. What's discernible from the contents of the auction was that Tiki had been more than just a business venture for him. His home had been built at the same time as the Polynesian Village, and by the same builders. Amongst the treasures salvaged from his home were the signature logo Tiki carving from Ren Clark's Polynesian Village, and a home Tiki bar complete with impressive wall diorama, puffer fish lamps, glass floats and bamboo galore. That he had held onto these and continued to live with all this long after the Polynesian Village's closing is testament to Clark's synergy with what he created.

Part of the allure of mid-century Tiki bars and restaurants was their weirdness and exoticism. It was an escapist paradise from the mundane day-to-day existence of the average citizen. Entering a Tiki bar, a suppressed mid-century American businessman in grey flannel suit could be transformed, for an evening, into a "suburban savage" - falling under the spell of pagan idols to the beat of native drums and the dance of mysterious native hula maidens whilst partaking in exotic cocktails and foods.

Like many other mid-century Tiki themed destinations, drinks at the Polynesian Village were served in specially designed cocktail vessels. There was a signature Tiki mug, based on the Tiki logo in which the "Tiki Ren" cocktail was served. The cocktail menu said of this drink "When you order the third one - we must have YOUR NEXT OF KIN" - a playful jest implying the potent nature of exotic drinks. Along with this cocktail container were three mugs shown on this page - the Fertility Goddess mug ("Black Woman" cocktail), a stylized Native mug (with the "Widowmaker" concoction) and the Wahine mug (which held a drink named "Virgin's Lament"). The cocktail menu pictured another serving container named the "Cannibal Bowl" - this one was a cauldron topped with a skull that served a large communal cocktail for four drinkers. It's as yet undocumented if this drink was actually served in this fashion, but with all that is known about Ren Clark's, it wouldn't be surprising in the least.

But by far the most coveted relic from Ren Clark's is the Severed Head mug. Ideally conjured for this venue whose drinking lounge was colorfully named the "Cannibal Room Cocktail Lounge", drinkers would imbibe the rum based "Headhunter's Special" cocktail from a ceramic mug resembling an upturned decapitated head, blood dripping down its sides with mouth agape in terror. The menu illustration depicts a native, based on an Igorot headhunter, wielding a knife in one hand and lopped-off head in the other.

Along similar lines, Tiki bar pioneer Trader Vic (Victor Bergeron) first introduced a skull mug in the 1940s that would thereafter be used at Tiki bars across the nation. A decade or so after Vic, the Mai Kai in Ft Lauderdale, Florida opened. Here select cocktails were served in a shrunken head mug. But neither Trader Vic's skull mug nor Mai Kai's shrunken head mug can quite match the sheer macabre and shocking nature of the Severed Head mug. In 2000 author Sven A Kirsten included photos of the mug in the pages of the bible of all things Tiki, *The Book of Tiki*, and introduced this rare artifact to Tiki aficionados worldwide. As a result it's since been one of the most sought after relics of the Polynesian Pop era. Reported sales on the secondary market have been as high as $1500, and there have been a number of nouveau mugs created by Tiki revivalist artists and mug makers in homage to Ren Clark's gruesome original.

Today, as with many aspects about Ren Clark's Polynesian Village, the exact conception of the Severed Head mug is still a mystery. It is reasonable to theorize that Clark, with his colorful and theatrical magical background, was instrumental (if not solely responsible) in the creation of this cocktail vessel. The fact that the Polynesian Village was only open for a ten year period - one could be forgiven that all this was just a alcohol fuelled mirage, but fortunately some evidence in the form of cocktail mugs, menus, and interior photos prove that such a magical oasis did indeed once exist. Perhaps one day a vintage photo will surface of a woman in a cocktail dress with beehive hairdo enjoying a "Headhunter's Special" from a Severed Head mug, and more of the picture of Ren Clark and his Polynesian Village will be revealed. Until then, it's best left to our imagination.

(from the food menu):

"day is done – enchantment beckons – the throbbing of muted drums heralds your arrival at a typical polynesian village ≠ where exotic viands and potations await – native chefs have been at work all day insuring a lavish repast for the returning hunters and warriors – you are invited to join in the revelry – formality is forgotten – indulgence is unlimited – soft breezes carry away care – tiki gods appease the war spirits - leaping flames and garish masks thwart the demons lurking in the trembling shadows – the tropic moon-filled night is for fun, and frantic passions abound – tomorrow is another day".

Cannibal Room Cocktail Lounge

These famous Polynesian drinks may be served ONLY if you have your own Rum or Beverage Locker.

BLACK WOMAN
A dusky belle from deep in the jungle. Sweeter than most, gets along with anything, but favors Vodka.
$1.25

PEARL DIVER
Plenty of lung capacity needed for this one. In each fifth drink served, comes a real pearl—best with Vodka or Gin.
$1.10

SKULLDUGGERY
Your taste buds will make no bones about this one. Favors Rum.
$1.15

WIDOWMAKER
Not actually a form of suicide, but you had better check with your insurance man—Scotch, Bourbon or Brandy.
$1.00

ALLIGATOR'S TAIL
Normally timid—when provoked, the alligator lashes out with a mighty swipe of his tail. Charged with Rum.
.90

VIRGIN'S LAMENT
You'll never resist one if sufficiently softened by enough of your favorite additive.
.75

PLANTER'S PUNCH
Yo ho ho and a bottle of Rum!
$1.25

CANNIBAL BOWL
For four or more hearty souls—should use Rum on this one but Scotch or Bourbon brings the same effect.
$5.00

ASK your attendant for an Application Blank for a LOCKER. Issued on an annual basis for $12.00.

Ren Clark's Polynesian Village
WESTERN HILLS HOTEL
FORT WORTH

All drinks shown here are Polynesian Village specialties, but should you wish another type, we will be happy to prepare the drink of your choice.

TIKI REN
Make this one your "Idol." When you order the third one—we must have your "NEXT OF KIN."
Favors Rum.
$1.25

PI-YI
Looks innocent enough but packs enough Rum to floor a mule.
$1.50

HEAD HUNTER'S SPECIAL
You'll lose your head over this one. Must be Rum.
$1.50

Ko-Ko-No-Ko KOOLER
A cool refreshing long one to dispel the heat of the day—mixes with Gin or Vodka.
$1.30

TIKI BOWL
The battle of the sexes recedes and man and his woman work together—mixes with most anything.
$1.15

NAVY GROG
A forthright blend of hairy chested Rum for men over 21.
$1.50

A KEY CLUB SPECIAL

SHIPWRECK
Appropriately named—suitable for hopeless castaways with no interest in further living—mixes with anything but turpentine.
$1.10

MAUNA LOA
The famous mountain of flowers blows its top every time it is provided with Rum.
$1.25

FOR THE YOUNG ONES:
Pieces of Eight
A Pirate's Treasure. Non-Alcoholic but not spiritless.
.50

BIG BAMBOO
If you're driving, better stop on three—try it with Rum.
.90

COPYRIGHT 1960–REN CLARK

(above) Drinks menu from the Cannibal Room Cocktail Lounge at Ren Clark's.

(opposite – clockwise from top left) Headhunter exoticism at its finest in the form of these cocktail vessels: a 1940s skull mug from Trader Vic's, a shrunken head mug from the Mai Kai, and two views of the Holy Grail – the one and only Severed Head mug from Ren Clark's. The base of the mug is stamped "Ren Clark's Polynesian Village" and features the maker's sticker - OMC (Otagiri Mercantile Company).

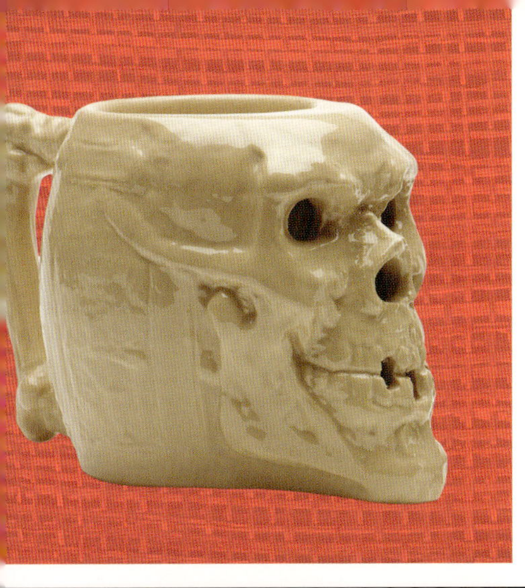

IN THE LAND OF MAKE BELIEVE

THE MAGIC KINGDOM OF BOBBY SHERMAN

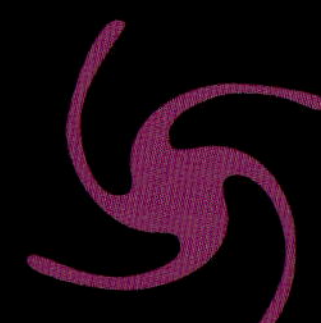

BY BOYD RICE

When evaluating the music of the late sixties and early seventies, rock critics have a tendency to give high marks to recordings featuring self indulgent jam sessions, guitar and drum solos, often dismissing the era's well crafted pop altogether. Which is a shame. What they fail to recognize is that the day's public took its pop very seriously. In 1968 the Monkees outsold the Beatles and Stones combined. In 1969 the Archies "Sugar Sugar" knocked the Rolling Stones out of the number one spot on the U.S. charts.

At about this same time a man appeared on the music scene who is perhaps one of the most underrated singer/songwriters of the era: Bobby Sherman. Bobby had good looks, sky blue eyes, an easy smile and a charisma that leapt off the TV screen or printed page. Not surprisingly he became a teen idol. Such status was undoubtedly both a blessing and curse to Sherman. His units moved by the ton, but it's doubtful that so called *serious* critics ever paid attention to what he was doing, if they listened at all. Surely, no one making music for 13 year old girls had anything of substance to say, right? Wrong.

Bobby Sherman was one of those rare individuals possessed of great passion and boundless curiosity. Though he started his career as a dancer on the TV show *Shindig*, he quickly learned how every piece of equipment on the set functioned. Later, as a recording artist, he built a studio in his home and would record a song he'd written playing every single instrument on the track. During a time when a lot of major groups had the Wrecking Crew do the music on their albums, Sherman was an auteur. Unlike a good many other teen idols, Bobby seems to have played a far more pivotal role in much of what he produced. His top 40 hits were masterpieces of pure pop, and can no more be denigrated or dismissed for being *mere* pop than any hit song from any era. But what's really interesting is the stuff Bobby did that defies all expectations. And there's quite a bit of it.

The paradox that defines much of Sherman's best material, is that he seems to have been a mystic creating music for an audience of *teeny-boppers*. In one song, Bobby sang the lyric that "You look for your own heaven and you live in your own hell / And you have to be your own Jesus". One wonders what 13 year old girls must have thought while listening to such lyrics. If William Blake had been a teen idol, he'd have been hard pressed to surpass such fare.

Sherman's best stuff was self written, or obviously hand selected by him. Some of it bore an eerie resemblance to songs on Charlie Manson's first album (recorded about the same time). On "Cease to Exist" Manson sang "Cease to exist / Just come and say you love me / Give up your world / Come on and be with me". On Bobby's mega-hit "Little Woman", he echoed such sentiments: "Hey little woman, please make up your mind / You've got to come into my world and leave your world behind". If anything, Bobby was even more messianic than the putative cult leader.

Decades before American terrorist Timothy McVeigh blew up the state building in Oklahoma City, Bobby did a song called "Oklahoma City Times". In it, he sings that he wants to *go out* "with not a whimper, but a bang". GO OUT?! Is he speaking of *death*? A teen idol extolling a glorious death? Evidently so. He goes on to explain that he wants his life to count for more than "just a few lines in The Oklahoma City Times".

When artists taken far more seriously were singing songs about peace and love, Bobby was composing minimalist pop masterpieces such as "Time": "Alone, I stand here alone", sings Bobby. Though he's surrounded by people, still he's alone. When trying to alert his peers to the spectre of *time*, he's laughed at. It is, of course, the price one pays to recognize what others can't. He continues:

Time, we all die from time
No matter who you are you answer to time
And I'll bet you a year
We are running out of time

As he looks into the mirror, he thinks it is lying to him, but he knows (of course) it's not.

Me. I trust only me
Everyone's tried once to make me see
But I can laugh too
As no one runs out on time. Time... Time...

At the time he wrote this song, Sherman undoubtedly felt isolated. He was an astute, obviously philosophical young man in his early twenties doing his best to elucidate his worldview, and express his feelings - and he did so well. Yet his audience would never quite understand how brilliant so much of it was, or even care. Nor would the day's critics. Bobby Sherman, even amidst such vast adulation was indeed, quite *alone*.

"In the Land of Make Believe" explores the blurring together of fantasy and reality, so as to make of them a single entity. For Bobby, it's a goal well within reach, even though it starts as a mere dream:

In the grass by my mind's blowing river
Tremblin' are the waters through my head
Makin' believe that you are here with me
Makin' believe
Makin' believe...

In Bobby's mind, the fantasy is so vivid he hears bells ringing, children playing and birds singing. In due course, his love is there with him and he takes his fantasy to the next level:

Here, you and me make believe
Make believe the world, isn't what we see
Hey, things ain't what they seem
Now come into my dream, and make believe with me

Yet again he invites the listener to come into his dream, abandon their world and live with him in what was elsewhere referred to as a "new forever". And again the entire vibe is surprisingly Manson-esque for a mere teen idol. But Bobby wasn't a *mere* teen idol, and that's the point.

His song "The Drum" compared the human heart to a drum, and featured the refrain:

All that is, is all
All that is, is all
I think I hear the drum

"ALL THAT IS, IS ALL"?!?! This was pretty heavy stuff coming from a man whose image adorned lunch boxes, wrist watches and black light posters. His songs were even released on acetates on the back of cereal boxes, and "The Drum" was amongst them.

Perhaps Bobby's strangest song was "Unborn Lullabye" featured on his last mainstream album:

You are sailing on a dark lake
Peaceful lake of time and love you've made
Soon you will know, what it is to grow
To search in doubt, only to search again
Let your mind be your captain
Let your body be your ship
As you come into the world to try again
You look for your own heaven
And you live in your own hell
And you've got to be your own Jesus...

Again, one had to wonder what his audience of teen-aged girls made of such fare. Were they ever listening to the lyrics, or were they distracted by his tight bell bottoms, paisley shirts, leather chokers and androgynous good looks?

Like all mystics operating in the pop idiom, Bobby sooner or later had to do a song about that ancient pagan subject, the Sun (Bardot did about 3 or so, didn't she?). In "Hey, Mr Sun", Sherman wakes up in the morning and says "Good morning, Sun!", deciding he has spent far too long looking at the world "through the raindrops". He's bored of chasing after something he can't find, of seeking his salvation in rainbows.

He says:

"Hey, Mr Sun, you can turn the night to day
You can chase away the rainbows, they're just illusions anyway".

In a time when rainbows were emblematic of peace and love, Sherman rejected them. He desired only that the Sun be his companion, tap him on the shoulders, and whisper in his ear. That should *walk with him* and *talk with him.*

Bobby first came to public attention when, as a child, he built a scale model of Disneyland in his backyard, and the story (featuring photos) appeared in a San Fernando Valley newspaper. Even then, the young Sherman exhibited a taste for the blurring together of fantasy and reality, as manifested in Walt Disney's theme park; and as later portrayed in so many of his songs.

Bobby Sherman's biography, in fact, kicks off at Disneyland. He and his biographer are observing fireworks high above The Magic Kingdom from the balcony of Club 33, a secret restaurant above Pirates of the Caribbean. The restaurant is so elite, that most consider it to be a mere urban legend. It is a place open to celebs like Michael Jackson, corporate executives and high ranking Freemasons. And Bobby has a lifetime membership there. Wait staff at the eatery recall Sherman with enthusiastic fondness, deeming him "one of the nicest men on earth".

In the U.S., where Sherman was an unrivaled teen superstar, he is perhaps most well remembered for elevating the leather choker to a kind of androgynous fashion trend (one that never went mainstream - though I sported one at the time). He was the direct antecedent to the David Cassidy phenomenon, and even had his own TV show in which he was a pop singer / songwriter touring the country in a *psychedelic hearse*! In real life, he toured in his own private jet, a plane he later sold to supergroup Led Zeppelin when first they began moving as many units as Bobby Sherman did.

What's been lost in the shuffle is Bobby's body of work, the best of which, arguably stands up to anything put out by Elvis, or Sinatra at that time. Some of it was pure fluff, of course, as much of pop tends to be. A lot of it, however, was above and beyond what most of his contemporaries had on offer. I, for one, love both equally. Both have much to offer the listener, and each constitute a component in the on-going paradox that is Bobby Sherman.

On the following pages we present a selection of paintings and drawings. Unless noted, all are from the Outré collection. Some are a sampling of works included in our forthcoming publication *Thrift Store Art*, edited by Boyd Rice and Martin McIntosh.

Gabriel Mayorga, Untitled, 1955,
oil on canvas,
24" x 12" / 61 x 30.5cm

Astley David Montague Cooper (1856-1924),
Who Enters Here,
1919, 56" x 36" / 142 x 91.5 cm,
oil on canvas in custom made frame.
(collection of Glenn Bray)

Roeger, Prometheus Bound and the Daughters of Neptune, 1959, oil on canvas, 20" x 24" / 51cm x 61cm

O. Patrian, Untitled, oil on canvas, 14" x 17 1/2" / 36cm x 44.5cm

Wolanozsk, Untitled, acrylic on canvas, 21 3/4" x 18" / 55cm x 46cm

W M H Kelly, Untitled, 1964, oil on canvas, 20" x 16" / 51cm x 41cm

W M H Kelly, Untitled, 1960, oil on canvas, 20" x 16" / 51cm x 41cm

(top) **M.J., Untitled,**
1957, graphite on paper,
8 3/4" x 6 1/4" / 22cm x 16cm

(bottom) **M.J., Untitled,**
1957, graphite on paper,
9" x 7 1/2" / 23cm x 19cm

Abruzzi, Untitled, oil on canvas, 20" x 16" / 51cm x 41cm

Jim Sinckland, Untitled, 1967,
oil on canvas board,
30" x 15" / 76cm x 38cm

J.J. Milam, Untitled, 1961, oil on canvas board, 8 1/2" x 6 1/2" / 21.5cm x 16.5cm

Remmel Roemheld Studio (label), **Untitled,** oil on canvas, 16" x 13 1/4" / 41cm x 33.5cm
(opposite) **Unsigned, Untitled**, oil on hessian, 16" x 12" / 41cm x 30.5cm

OUTRÉ JOURNAL READERS

SIMCA
Imported from Paris

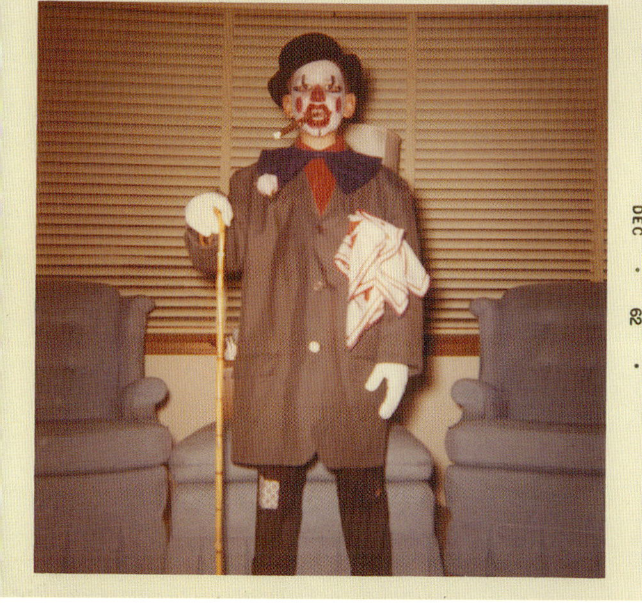
DEC • 62 •

PLEASE DO NOT TOUCH

MUSIC FOR ROBOTS

Contributors

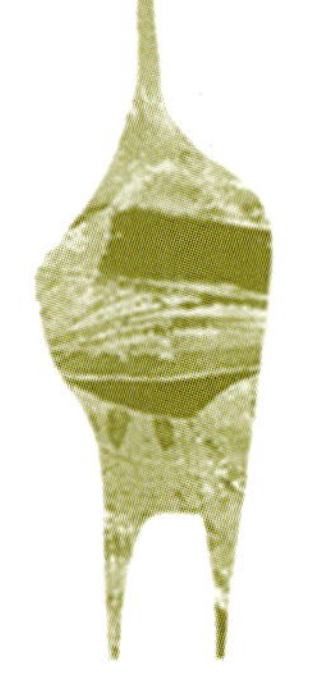

Photo: Lille Smallwood

Brian Chidester is the co-author of *Pop Surf Culture: Music, Design, Film and Fashion from the Bohemian Surf Era* (Santa Monica Press) and the co-editor of *Dumb Angel* magazine. He currently lives in New York City and writes for the *Village Voice*.

Boyd Rice has been known over the last several decades as an Avant-garde recording artist, and co-founder of the genre known as Industrial Music. As a writer, his output has appeared in upwards of a half dozen languages. Recent books include *NO* and the novel *Twilight Man*, based upon his experiences in San Francisco during the Eighties. His most recent recording, *Back to Mono*, will be out later in the year on Mute Records. He currently resides in an underground bunker in Denver, Colorado that includes a room with a Bacchus theme complemented with metallic silver walls, zebra carpets and black butterfly chairs.

Photo: Robin

Photo: Clément Boulland

Jean-Emmanuel Deluxe is a writer and performer. He collaborated for several US & UK magazines (*Roctober, Shindig*) along with several publications from his homeland (including *Playboy*). He recently finished a book on French pop girls for Feral House. He runs the label Martyrs of pop which has released recordings by many varied artists including April March, Leatherman (Jacques Duvall & Jean-Marc Lederman) & Alexander Faem. With a documentary planned, a TV show, a comic book with the great Bart Johnson and reissues of French pop & rock classics on the way he realizes everyday that the possibilities are endless and suggests not eating the same cultural dish everyday!

Charles Schneider has spent his life exploring the realms of the macabre with a mercurial, and sometimes, comedic twist. His weird horror stories are gaining recognition by connoisseurs and major creators in the horror genre, with the publication of *The Mauve Embellishments*, a collection of stories and art. His film work is filled with similar dark visions of odd dream-like places. Schneider's artwork matches this decadently playful aesthetic. In fact, he was chosen to paint the "death portraits" in the film *Art School Confidential*. As a character actor, his face and voice are equally distinct. He edits books about obscure and forgotten aspects of popular culture, such as *Burlesque Paraphernalia*. He has shared his love of beautiful, heartfelt folk music by producing several albums by the late Utah musician, Bob Moss. He is an accomplished magician, favoring atmospheric stories to punctuate his illusions. Read more at www.charlesschneiderproductions.com

Martin McIntosh resides in Melbourne, Australia where he is the director of Outré Gallery. He has edited a number of books including *Taboo: The Art of Tiki, Supersonic Swingers* and *Beatsville*. Once a month he can be found playing records with Mai Tai in hand at Melbourne's LuWow tiki bar. He enjoys dusty secondhand bookshops, junk stores and spending time with his family. He one day hopes to open a museum with an outré slant.

Nicholas Syracuse has exhibited at numerous galleries across the US. He has a solo show at the F+Gallery in Los Angeles opening October 1st this year. Syracuse's photograph "Infinity Birds, NYC" has been chosen by Bobby Beausoleil to be the cover for his upcoming album release. When not photographing throughout America, he lives and works in New York City. Prints of his Black House photographs are available for purchase directly from him. Contact: nsyracuse@gmail.com